ABRIDGED EDITION

Sunset Cook Book for
Entertaining

By the Editors of Sunset Books *and* Sunset Magazine

LANE BOOKS · MENLO PARK, CALIFORNIA

Introduction

This book is dedicated to providing the ultimate in dining delight for your guests, and the maximum of leisure and pleasure for you, the hostess.

Three main features are aimed at helping you prepare a wide variety of sumptuous foods with a minimum of worry and fluster:
- Recipes unique enough for special entertaining, but also sufficiently easy and convenient to make.
- Tested menus and party plans suitable for many different occasions.
- Guides and tips for adding those special touches and embellishments which transform an ordinary get-together into a memorable event.

To plan your own menus, you may select from the large variety of individual recipes on pages 4 through 63. Most of these dishes are much easier to make than the glamorous results indicate, and many may be made entirely in advance. Menus and party plans, with appropriate recipes, will be found on pages 64 through 93. These range from very simple and informal get-togethers to bountiful and elegant affairs. You may follow these plans exactly, modify them by making suggested substitutions, or use the menus to inspire your own ideas.

Each menu and recipe in this book has been prepared and tested by the home economics department of *Sunset Magazine.*

Illustrations by Alyson Smith

Cover Photograph by Glenn Christiansen. Danish Chicken and Meatballs au Gratin, page 29.

First Printing September 1971

Copyright © Lane Magazine & Book Company, Menlo Park, California. Second Edition 1971. World rights reserved.

Contents

Appealing Appetizers

IN ALMOST EVERY COUNTRY, appetizers typical of the native cuisine are used for snacks or a special beginning to meals. But in the United States, ideas have been adopted from all over the world with some typically American innovations added. These recipes reflect the international tastes of people in the United States, yet present choices for those who prefer less exotic combinations. Most are easy to prepare completely or partially ahead.

A large part of the chapter consists of recipes that can be served to guests in the living room, on the patio, or wherever they are socializing before dinner. Many are suitable snacks for entertaining when you are not serving a complete meal.

The last group of recipes is for first-course or "sit-down" appetizers, usually presented on individual plates and eaten with a fork at the dinner table. Some are particularly attractive; you may wish to have them waiting as an appetizing greeting for guests when they come to the table.

Guacamole

This version of a Western favorite has two new flavor additions—chopped pimiento (which also adds color) and coriander, a frequently used spice in Mexico.

Garnish the guacamole with tomato wedges and parsley, and serve it with corn chips or crisp fried tortillas.

    2   large ripe avocados
    3   tablespoons lime juice
    4   canned California green chiles, seeded,
          rinsed, and chopped
    1   canned pimiento, chopped
    ¾   teaspoon ground coriander
        About ½ teaspoon salt, or to taste
        Tomato wedges
        Parsley

Peel and pit avocados and mash coarsely with a fork. Blend in lime juice, chiles, pimiento, coriander, and salt to taste. Garnish with tomato wedges and parsley. Makes 6 to 8 servings for individual portions, more if used as a dip.

Refried Bean Dip

Bland refried beans become a tasty dip-type appetizer when heated with cheese, onion, and taco sauce.

    1   can (1 lb.) refried beans
    1   cup (¼ lb.) shredded Cheddar cheese
    ½   cup chopped green onion (including part
          of the tops)
    ¼   teaspoon salt
    2   to 3 tablespoons canned taco sauce
        Crisp fried tortillas or tortilla chips

Mix beans, cheese, onion, salt, and taco sauce in a small pan or heatproof Mexican pottery bowl. Cook over coals, stirring, until heated. Keep warm on barbecue, or use chafing dish. Serve with crisp fried tortillas, or tortilla chips. Makes about 3 cups.

CRISP FRIED TORTILLAS. Heat about 1 inch of salad oil in a frying pan over medium-high heat. Cut about a dozen tortillas each into 6 pie-shaped pieces. Fry about 8 at a time, turning occasionally, until crisp and lightly browned, about 2 minutes. Drain on paper towels; sprinkle lightly with salt if desired.

Raw Radish Dip

This crunchy red radish dip is refreshing served with corn chips, other sturdy chips, or crackers.

- 1 large package (8 oz.) cream cheese, softened
- 1 tablespoon lemon juice
- ¼ teaspoon dill weed
- 1 teaspoon salt
- 1 clove garlic, mashed
- 1 cup chopped radishes

In a small bowl, blend together cream cheese, lemon juice, dill weed, salt, and garlic. Add chopped radishes and stir until blended. Cover; refrigerate for at least 2 hours. You might garnish with a radish rose and parsley. Makes about 2 cups.

Onion-Dill Dip

This dill dip complements all raw vegetables, including the more unfamiliar flavors of raw green bean, zucchini, turnip, or asparagus.

- 2½ cups regular or low-fat plain yogurt
- 1 package (amount for 4 servings) dry onion soup mix
- 1 tablespoon minced parsley
- ¼ teaspoon garlic powder
- 1 teaspoon dill weed
- Dash pepper

Combine all ingredients. Chill at least 1 hour to blend flavors. Serve with cherry tomatoes; pieces of crisp vegetables such as carrots, celery, radishes, or cauliflower; or some of the more unusual vegetables suggested above. Makes about 3 cups.

Cheddar Cheese Spread

This cheese spread is handy to have around for unexpected visitors. It keeps for several months and also can be used to top hot soup, vegetables, baked potatoes, and home-baked breads.

- 1 pound each aged sharp and mild Cheddar cheese
- 2 cloves garlic, crushed
- 2 tablespoons Worcestershire
- 1 teaspoon each salt and dry mustard
- ⅛ teaspoon liquid hot-pepper seasoning
- 1 cup beer

Cut cheese into ¼-inch slices and put into the large bowl of your electric mixer. Let stand at room temperature for 4 to 6 hours, or until very soft. Beat until light-colored and smooth. Add garlic, Worcestershire, salt, dry mustard, and liquid hot-pepper seasoning, and blend thoroughly. Add beer ¼ cup at a time, blending well after each addition, and continue beating until light and fluffy. Store in covered jars in the refrigerator. Makes 1½ quarts.

Shrimp-Stuffed Tomatoes

Bite-sized stuffed tomatoes are so neat to eat that neither toothpick nor napkin accompaniment is needed. They are ideal for large groups.

- 1 basket cherry tomatoes
- ½ pound cooked, shelled shrimp
- 1 green onion, chopped
- 3 or 4 pitted black olives, chopped
- 1 tablespoon soy sauce

Wash and drain tomatoes; cut a thin slice off the top of each and scoop out the pulp. Invert the tomatoes and set aside to drain. Chop the shrimp very fine and combine with the onion, olives, and soy sauce. Stuff this mixture into the tomato shells and refrigerate up to 6 hours. Makes 2½ dozen.

Chilled Asparagus Spears

Green spears of cold fresh asparagus, if cooked just until tender but still firm, make marvelous finger food to serve with dip. The spears look especially elegant standing upright in a crystal goblet or bowl. Allow 3 to 6 spears per serving.

- 2 pounds fresh asparagus spears
- 3 cups rich meat stock
- 1 carrot, thinly sliced
- 1 lemon, thinly sliced (do not peel)
- 3 sprigs parsley
- 1 tablespoon diced onion
- 1 teaspoon salt

Trim asparagus spears to the same length. In a wide shallow pan bring to a boil meat stock seasoned with carrot, lemon, parsley, onion, and salt. Add asparagus, keeping spears parallel, and cook covered just until tender. Chill in stock. Drain spears, and place upright in a bowl or flat on a tray; serve with Browned Butter Mayonnaise.

BROWNED BUTTER MAYONNAISE. Heat ½ pound (1 cup) butter until richly browned. Remove from heat and let cool slightly. Beat 4 egg yolks until thick. Add warm butter 2 tablespoonsful at a time, beating constantly with a rotary beater (or whirl yolks in a blender for a few seconds, then add butter in a slow, steady stream). Serve immediately, or chill and whip to soften before serving. Makes about 1½ cups.

Marinated Mushrooms

Fresh sliced raw mushrooms are marinated with oil, vinegar, and tarragon.

    1   pound uniform mushrooms
    ¾   cup olive oil
    3   tablespoons tarragon vinegar
    ½   teaspoon salt
         A little freshly ground black pepper
    2   teaspoons minced parsley
    ½   teaspoon minced fresh or dried tarragon

Wash mushrooms and slice them lengthwise, right through stem and cap. Combine other ingredients and mix well with mushrooms. Let stand 5 or 6 hours before serving (don't chill).

Ginger-Minted Carrots

Tangy with orange and ginger, these tiny cooked carrots brighten an assortment of less colorful appetizers and provide a low-calorie choice.

    3   packages (10 oz. each) frozen baby carrots
    1   cup orange juice
    1   teaspoon grated fresh ginger
         Dash each salt and pepper
    1   tablespoon chopped fresh mint

Combine carrots, orange juice, ginger, salt, and pepper in pan. Cover and bring to boil; simmer until carrots are just tender, about 3 minutes. Chill carrots, covered in liquid. Drain and spoon into serving bowl; garnish carrots with mint. Serve with picks. Makes 6 cups.

Cucumber-Cheese Slices

These cheese and olive-filled cucumber slices have all the virtues of a good appetizer: They look beautiful, taste good, are easy to prepare, may be made ahead, and whet the appetite rather than satiate.

    2   packages (3 oz. each) soft chive cream cheese
    ¼   cup finely chopped pimiento-stuffed olives,
         well drained
    4   small, thin cucumbers (about 5 inches long),
         peeled

Blend cream cheese with olives. Cut tapered ends off each cucumber and hollow by scooping out all the seeds with a knife or apple corer. Pack the hollow of each solidly with a fourth of the cream cheese mixture. Wrap each cucumber in plastic film, and chill thoroughly. Cut crosswise in ⅓-inch slices. Makes about 60 slices.

Indonesian Broiled Chicken

A classic Indonesian entrée has been adapted to a skewered appetizer which broils so quickly that even a hungry guest may enjoy cooking his own. You can prepare the skewers with nut and lime coating ahead.

    2   whole chicken breasts
    1   package (8 oz.) broken walnuts (2 cups)
    ⅔   cup lime juice
    2   tablespoons chicken stock or broth
    2   green onions, cut up
    2   small cloves garlic, mashed
    ½   teaspoon salt
    1   cup yogurt or sour cream

Cut the uncooked chicken from the bones in bite-sized pieces and set aside. Combine the nuts, lime juice, chicken stock, onions, garlic, and salt in an electric blender and whirl until the nuts are quite fine. Mix ½ cup of this nut mixture with the yogurt or sour cream to serve as a dip with the chicken; chill thoroughly.

Gently coat the pieces of chicken with the remaining nut mixture and refrigerate for 2 to 3 hours. Then string the coated chicken pieces on skewers and refrigerate until you are ready to cook the meat. Broil or grill the chicken about 5 inches from the source of heat for 5 to 7 minutes, turning once. Serve with the reserved sauce. Makes 8 to 10 skewers.

Hawaiian Beef Sticks

These "meat sticks" are a classic in Hawaii; they are a kebab variation of beef teriyaki with the sauce thickened so it won't drip off during broiling.

         A 2-inch piece fresh ginger, sliced
    2   cloves garlic, mashed
    2   small onions, chopped
    1   cup soy sauce
    4   tablespoons sugar
    8   small, dried, hot chile peppers
    2   tablespoons red wine vinegar
    4   teaspoons cornstarch
    ½   cup water
    2   pounds beef sirloin

In a small pan, combine fresh ginger, garlic, onions, soy sauce, sugar, chile peppers, and vinegar. Cook over medium heat until slightly thick, about 20 minutes. Combine cornstarch with water. Gradually stir into sauce and cook, stirring until clear and thickened. Pour mixture through a wire strainer, pressing out all juices, and discard the pulp; cool. Cut beef into bite-sized pieces; add to marinade and allow to stand, covered, for 2 hours. Thread 2 or 3 pieces of meat on each skewer; barbecue over hot coals or broil. Makes 4 dozen.

Sweet-Sour Sausage Balls

This Hawaiian recipe uses a Chinese sweet and sour sauce spiked with a liberal amount of native American catsup. Especially suitable for serving a crowd, the meatballs are economical and easy to prepare, freeze, and reheat.

4	pounds bulk pork sausage
4	eggs, slightly beaten
1½	cups soft bread crumbs
3	cups catsup
¾	cup brown sugar, firmly packed
½	cup each white wine vinegar and soy sauce

Mix together sausage, eggs, and bread crumbs. Using palms of hands, shape mixture into balls the size of small walnuts. Sauté in frying pan until browned on all sides; drain. Combine catsup, brown sugar, vinegar, and soy sauce; pour over sausage balls and simmer 30 minutes, stirring occasionally. Serve hot. (If made ahead, refrigerate or freeze sausage balls in their sauce. To serve, reheat in a 350° oven for 20 minutes.) Makes 150 balls.

Quiche Lorraine Appetizers

This variation of the classic *quiche* is baked in a shallow rectangular pan, rather than in the customary pie shape. This is so you can cut it into squares to serve as hot appetizers, either on napkins or little plates. You may also serve it as a first course at the table. The quiche has an egg pastry base with cheese and bacon custard topping.

	Pastry (recipe follows)
14	slices cooked bacon, finely chopped
1¼	cups (about 6 oz.) diced or thinly sliced Swiss cheese
4	eggs
1¼	cups heavy cream
½	cup milk
	Freshly grated nutmeg (or ground nutmeg)

Make the pastry (recipe follows) and roll to fit a 10 by 15-inch rimmed shallow baking pan. Fit pastry flush with the top edge of pan and trim evenly if necessary. Prick bottom in about 20 places with fork. Bake in a 425° oven for 12 to 15 minutes, or until lightly browned. Cool. Wrap airtight if not used soon.

Evenly distribute bacon and cheese over the bottom of the pastry shell. Beat eggs until they are blended, then mix well with cream and milk. Pour liquid over the cheese and bacon. Grate a little nutmeg over the filling.

Bake in a 325° oven for 25 minutes or until filling appears set when gently shaken (if it puffs, prick with a fork to allow air to escape). Cut in small squares and serve while very hot. (This does not reheat well.) Makes 40 pieces about 2 inches square.

PASTRY. Measure 1½ cups unsifted all-purpose flour into a bowl. Add ⅛ teaspoon salt and 9 tablespoons (½ cup plus 1 tablespoon) butter, cut in small pieces. With a pastry blender or your fingers break the butter into very small particles; the largest should be the size of small peas. Beat 1 egg and add to flour mixture, blending well with a fork. Shape mixture with your hands to form a compact ball.

Roll dough out on a well floured board; turn dough occasionally to prevent sticking. Gently fit pastry into pan (if it tears, just press edges together).

Tostadas de Harina
TORTILLAS WITH BROILED CHEESE

In Mexico the tortillas for Tostadas de Harina are made a giant size. Regular-sized flour tortillas (7 inches in diameter) will work equally well. You can prepare the tostadas for baking several hours ahead.

6	flour tortillas
2	cups shredded mild Cheddar cheese
2	tablespoons chopped, seeded, canned California green chiles

Evenly sprinkle tortillas with cheese, leaving about a ½-inch margin around edges. Top with chiles. Bake on ungreased baking sheets in a 425° oven for 8 to 10 minutes or until edges are crisp and browned. Cut each tortilla into 6 wedges; serve hot. Makes 36 wedges.

Coquilles St. Jacques

The most simple version of this classic is merely wine-poached scallops with parsley butter sauce. Its simplicity requires interesting serving dishes, either scallop shells or individual casseroles.

1½	pounds scallops
1½	cups dry white wine (or ¾ cup wine and ¾ cup water)
½	cup (¼ lb.) melted butter
2	tablespoons chopped parsley
	Paprika

Wash and drain scallops. Put them in a pan with wine and water, if used. Bring liquid to a boil, cover, reduce heat, and simmer for 8 to 10 minutes. Remove scallops and cut them in large slices.

Arrange the sliced scallops in 4 shells or individual casseroles. Spoon 2 tablespoons melted butter over top of each filled shell. Sprinkle 1½ teaspoons parsley over each, then sprinkle them with paprika and heat in a 350° oven for 5 minutes. Makes 4 servings.

Stuffed Clam Appetizers

Here the French way of preparing *escargots* (snails) with garlic butter sauce has been adapted to small clams. Littleneck or butter clams are bountiful, and the shells hold plenty of delicious sauce.

2	dozen clams
2	tablespoons water
¼	cup (⅛ lb.) soft butter
1	large clove garlic, minced or mashed
2	tablespoons finely chopped parsley
3	tablespoons fresh bread crumbs (whirl about ½ slice bread in blender) or 1 tablespoon fine dry bread crumbs

Put well-scrubbed clams in a large pan with the 2 tablespoons water; heat just until the shells open. When cool enough to handle, remove whole clams from shells; save half the shells.

Combine butter, garlic, parsley, and bread crumbs. Set each clam back on a half shell, spread with about 1 teaspoonful of the butter mixture, and arrange on a baking pan. (You can do this much ahead, then cover and refrigerate until time to serve them.) Set the clams about 4 inches from broiler unit and broil until lightly browned, 3 to 4 minutes. Makes 24.

Artichokes Vinaigrette

Bits of pimiento, pickle, and parsley brighten this dish made from frozen artichoke hearts. They star as the first course at dinner.

1	package (9 oz.) frozen artichoke hearts or 2 cups fresh trimmed and halved artichoke hearts
	Boiling salted water
6	tablespoons olive oil
2	tablespoons red wine vinegar
3	tablespoons minced sweet pickle
1	tablespoon sweet pickle liquid
2	tablespoons each minced parsley and pimiento

Cook artichokes in boiling salted water as directed on package or until tender. Drain and place in a small deep bowl. Pour over them the olive oil and vinegar. Gently mix in the pickle, pickle liquid, parsley, and pimiento. Cover and chill at least 4 hours or overnight. Lift artichokes from marinade and arrange 6 to 8 halves on each individual plate. With a slotted spoon, remove some of the chopped ingredients from marinade and spoon over the artichoke hearts. Makes 4 servings.

SIMPLE BUT SPECIAL APPETIZERS

The easiest appetizers are those from can or bottle. However, with little effort, you can prepare some of the following simple and beautiful tidbits, which reflect the attention to detail for which good hosts and hostesses are known.

Crudités (French-style raw vegetables) with Homemade Mayonnaise Dip. Fill a small straw basket with a "nosegay" of fresh, raw relish vegetables such as cauliflower, Chinese (edible pod) peas, baby carrots, radishes, artichoke hearts, cherry tomatoes, cucumber, asparagus spears, green beans, and celery. Cut large vegetables into sticks, slivers, or other easy-to-dip shapes.

To make mayonnaise, place in a blender 1 egg, ½ teaspoon *each* sugar and paprika, 1 teaspoon Dijon-style mustard, and 3 tablespoons tarragon-flavored white wine vinegar. Blend a few seconds, and with motor running gradually pour in 1 cup salad oil, blending until smooth.

Edam Cheese Balls. Slice 1½ inches off the top of an Edam cheese and use a melon ball cutter to scoop out balls. Refill the cheese shell with the balls.

Fennel and Blue Cheese. Arrange cheese on a bed of fennel leaves on tray. Add pieces of crisp raw fennel stalk. Provide knives for spreading cheese on fennel.

Melon with Meat. Cut melon into bite-sized chunks and wrap with a paper-thin slice of one of the appropriate meats suggested. Fasten with toothpicks. Persian, Crenshaw, and Casaba melons and honeydew or cantaloupe are all complemented by prosciutto, Westphalian ham, and baked ham. Other meats which match well with most melons are pastrami, corned beef, tongue, smoked beef, Canadian bacon, Genoa or dry salami, smoked thuringer, Lebanon bologna, galantina, mortadella, and coppa.

Cream Cheese Trio. Arrange 3 packages (3 oz. *each*) cream cheese on narrow tray. Coat 1 block with toasted sesame seed, drizzle soy sauce over top. Press chopped chives into second cheese block to cover all of the surfaces generously. Spoon canned taco sauce over third cheese block; add additional sauce as required.

Serve with crisp crackers.

Curried Almonds. Use blanched or unblanched almonds. (To dry recently blanched almonds, spread them in a pan and bake in a 300° oven for 20 or 30 minutes.)

Heat ¼ cup salad oil in large frying pan. Add 2 pounds almonds; sprinkle with 2 tablespoons curry powder. Sauté, stirring, until nicely colored. Sprinkle with salt and drain on paper towels.

Melon Appetizer

This simple melon cocktail should look as good as it tastes. Pile it in a crystal bowl, or even a vase, with a few lime slices. Or make individual servings in tall stemmed goblets, brandy snifters, or hollowed melon halves. Be imaginative with garnish.

    1   each medium-sized Crenshaw melon and
            medium-sized Persian melon
    2   tablespoons lime juice (or juice of
            1 large lime)
    2   tablespoons honey
    ¼   teaspoon each ground coriander and nutmeg

Cut melons in halves, remove and discard seeds. Cut fruit into balls of different sizes, using melon (or French) ball cutter, or metal measuring spoons. Place fruit and all juices in a deep bowl. Mix together lime juice, honey, coriander, and nutmeg. Blend with the melon. Cover and chill. Spoon into serving bowls. Makes 8 to 10 servings.

Fettucine

NOODLES IN CREAM AND CHEESE

In Italy pasta is customarily served as a first course. Preparing *fettucine* at the table provides a dramatic beginning to your dinner. Before the eyes of your guests you toss egg noodles with butter, cream, and Parmesan in a chafing dish. Those who shrink from exhibitionism may perform in the kitchen and still reap ovations.

    3   cups hot boiled tagliarini or egg noodles
            (packaged or freshly made)
        Hot water
    6   tablespoons butter
    1¼ cups heavy cream
    1   cup shredded Parmesan cheese
        Salt and pepper
        Fresh grated nutmeg (or ground nutmeg)

Keep the noodles warm after cooling by floating in water that is hot to touch. In a wide frying pan or chafing dish over high heat on a range, melt butter until it is lightly browned. Add ½ cup of the cream and boil rapidly until large shiny bubbles form; stir occasionally. (Do this ahead, then reheat.)

Reduce heat to medium or place chafing dish over direct flame. Drain noodles well and add to the sauce. Toss vigorously with 2 forks, and pour in the cheese and the remaining cream, a little at a time—about three additions.

Season with salt and pepper and grate nutmeg generously over the noodles (or use about ⅛ teaspoon of the ground spice). Serve immediately. Makes 4 to 6 servings.

Antipasto Platter

Italian vegetable antipasto in decorative glass jars is sold by gourmet shops at high prices; for a fraction of the cost, you can make the same thing. The home-made version will be just as attractive if you cut the vegetables in uniform shapes. Many vegetables in addition to those mentioned in the recipe can be used, such as artichoke hearts, tiny onions, and green beans.

    1   cup each catsup, chile sauce, and water
    ½   cup each olive oil, tarragon vinegar, and
            lemon juice
    1   clove garlic, minced or mashed
    2   tablespoons brown sugar
    1   tablespoon each Worcestershire and
            prepared horseradish
        Salt to taste
        Dash of cayenne
    ½   head cauliflower
    3   medium-sized carrots
    2   stalks celery
    ½   pound small whole mushrooms
    1   jar (8 oz.) peperoncini (small peppers),
            drained
    2   cans (7 oz. each) solid pack tuna
    1   can (2 oz.) rolled anchovies with capers
        Pimiento-stuffed olives
        Parsley

Combine in a large pan the catsup, chile sauce, water, oil, vinegar, and lemon juice. Season with garlic, brown sugar, Worcestershire, horseradish, salt, and cayenne. Bring to a boil and simmer a few minutes.

Cut cauliflower into flowerets, peel and slice carrots, and slice celery diagonally into 1½-inch pieces. Add to the sauce the cauliflowerets, carrots, celery, mushrooms, and peppers; simmer slowly for 20 minutes, or until crisp-tender. Add drained tuna and simmer a few minutes longer.

Spoon into divided dishes, keeping each kind of vegetable and fish together. Cool and then chill. Garnish with anchovies, sliced olives, and parsley. Makes 10 to 12 servings.

Soups and Salads

AFTER THE APPETIZERS, and before the the main dish of a meal, you may want to serve a soup or a salad or both, beginning with the soup. At some meals you may prefer to serve the salad with or after the entrée. This chapter gives you enough recipes for both soups and salads to enable you to make an appropriate choice.

The soups range from clear, light ones for beginning a meal to heartier versions. Some cold soups are included, which can be delicious in hot weather or a nice contrast after a hot appetizer. Most are simple and easy to make. Suggestions for colorful toppings and garnishes are found on page 12.

Although a tossed green salad is always appreciated, new and different salad recipes are included, plus interesting variation on old stand-bys. Some of these salads reflect an interest in foods of many nations; others just demonstrate an imaginative approach to salad-making.

Tips for making tossed salads and a reminder list of greens and other colorful salad ingredients are also included.

Main-dish soups and salads will be found in the Entrées chapter.

Iced Tomato Soup

You'll appreciate the magic an electric blender can work with simple ingredients when you make this quick cold soup out of nothing but canned tomatoes and a few subtle seasonings.

> 1   can (1 lb. 12 oz.) pear-shaped tomatoes
> 1½ tablespoons lemon juice
> 1   bay leaf
> 1   chile pequin (or ½ small dried hot chile pepper)
> 1   teaspoon salt
>   Dash ground cumin
> 1   strip orange peel
>   Chopped green onions

In a 5-cup electric blender container, combine tomatoes, lemon juice, bay leaf, chile pepper, salt, cumin, and orange peel (peel orange with vegetable peeler). Whirl smooth; garnish with chopped green onions, if you wish, and serve cold. Makes 5 to 6 servings.

Chilled Beet Soup

This borscht-type soup, to be sipped cold, is made in minutes in a blender. You can present it elegantly if you pour the soup into mugs or clear punch cups and nestle them in a bowl of crushed ice.

> 1   can (1 lb.) sliced beets
> 1   can (14 oz.) regular strength beef broth
> 3   tablespoons lemon juice
> 1½ tablespoons honey
> ⅛   teaspoon each caraway seed and salt
> 1   whole clove
>   Sour cream
>   Chopped green onion

In a 5-cup electric blender container, combine beets and their liquid, broth, lemon juice, honey, caraway seed, salt, and clove. Whirl smooth and chill. Stir before serving. Garnish each serving with sour cream and a little chopped green onion. Makes 6 servings.

Pacific Gazpacho

Icy cold *gazpacho* (gaz-*pah*-cho) is a soupy salad or salad-like soup, whichever way you want to regard it. Originated by Spanish peasants, the classic (containing chopped cucumbers, onion, tomatoes, and garlic) is thinned with ice water, olive oil, and lemon juice or vinegar, then topped with bread cubes or crumbs. Many variations have been devised, such as this Pacific Gazpacho with avocado, sour cream, and bacon.

  6   medium-sized tomatoes
  2   cups canned condensed beef broth
  ½   teaspoon basil
  3   tablespoons lemon or lime juice
  2   tablespoons olive oil
  ½   cup finely diced sweet onion
  1   large avocado, peeled, pitted, and cubed
      Salt
      Avocado slices
      Thinly sliced onion rings
      Sour cream
  6   slices cooked bacon
      Ice cubes

Peel tomatoes and cut them in large pieces, saving the juice. Whirl smooth in a blender with beef broth. (Or chop the tomatoes very finely and blend with the broth.) Blend in basil, lemon or lime juice, olive oil, and onion. Gently stir in cubed avocado. Add salt if needed; the broth is usually salty enough. Chill thoroughly.

Ladle soup into shallow bowls. To each serving add several avocado slices, onion rings, about 1 tablespoon sour cream, 1 slice crumbled crisp bacon, and a few ice cubes. Makes 6 servings.

Wine Consommé

A dry red wine such as Cabernet or Zinfandel perfumes classic beef consommé. The soup can be served hot, cold, or jellied. Lemon serves both as a garnish and taste addition.

  4   cups regular strength beef stock
  1   egg white, slightly beaten
  1   cup dry red wine
  1   teaspoon sugar
      Dash lemon juice
      Salt and pepper
      Thin lemon slices

Heat beef stock to boiling point. To clarify it, stir in the egg white, and bring mixture to a boil; strain through a moistened muslin cloth, discard egg white, and return clarified stock to the pan. Bring again to a boil, and add wine, sugar, and lemon juice. Add salt and pepper to taste. Serve hot garnished with lemon slices. Makes 6 servings.

VARIATION: JELLIED CONSOMMÉ. Soften 2 packages unflavored gelatin in ½ cup water. Add gelatin mixture to boiling clarified stock (see preceding recipe) along with wine, sugar, and lemon juice; chill until set. Whip with a fork and serve with lemon wedges.

Avocado Bouillon

Hot chicken broth and clam juice, flavored with Sherry or lemon, contains cubes of avocado. A topping of whipped cream, parsley, and paprika is colorful if you choose to serve it for the holidays.

  1   can (10½ oz.) condensed chicken broth
  1   soup can water
  ½   cup canned or bottled clam juice
  1   medium-sized or 2 small avocados
      Salt to taste
  2   tablespoons Sherry or lemon juice
      About ½ cup cream, whipped
      Finely chopped parsley
      Paprika

Combine chicken broth, water, and clam juice. Heat piping hot. Meanwhile, peel and cube the avocados; spoon into each bouillon cup. Sprinkle with salt. Just before removing broth from heat, add Sherry. Pour over avocado cubes in cups. Top each with whipped cream and garnish with parsley and paprika. Serve immediately, with salted crackers, if you wish. Makes 4 to 6 servings.

Chicken - Cucumber Soup

Chopped cucumbers and fresh ginger root give this chicken soup a fresh-as-spring flavor. You can increase the amount of white wine in some servings to suit individual tastes.

  2   large cucumbers, peeled
  2   tablespoons butter or margarine
  5   cups chicken stock or canned chicken broth
        (regular strength)
  ½   teaspoon grated fresh ginger
  1   green onion, thinly sliced
      Salt and pepper
  ½   cup dry white wine (Chablis or Sauterne)
      Cucumber slices

Cut cucumbers into quarters, remove seeds, and chop finely. Sauté chopped cucumbers in butter for about 1 minute. Add chicken stock, ginger, and onion. Season to taste with salt and pepper. Simmer for about 15 minutes. Stir in wine and reheat quickly. Garnish with thin cucumber slices. Makes 6 servings.

Les Halles Onion Soup Gratinée

Countless bowls of this onion soup have been served in the cafes of the Les Halles district of Paris, once the site of the city's wholesale produce market. You can prepare the soup up to a day ahead, then bake it just before serving.

6	large yellow onions, thinly sliced
2	tablespoons butter or margarine
1	tablespoon olive oil
6	cups canned beef broth
	Salt and pepper to taste
⅓	cup white or red Port
½	cup diced Gruyère or Danish Samsoe cheese
6	slices buttered, dry toasted French bread, sliced ½ inch thick
1	cup mixed shredded Gruyère and Parmesan cheeses
1	tablespoon melted butter

Use a heavy-bottomed 3 or 4-quart covered pan. Sauté onions in butter and oil until limp. Cover and let simmer slowly for 15 minutes. Pour in beef broth and simmer for 30 minutes. Taste, and add salt and pepper if needed. Pour soup and the Port into an ovenproof earthenware casserole, cover, and heat in a 350° oven for 30 minutes.

Remove from oven and sprinkle with the diced Gruyère cheese. Cover with an even layer of toasted French bread and sprinkle with the shredded cheeses. Dribble over the melted butter. Return to 425° oven for 10 minutes, then turn on the broiler and heat just until the cheese browns lightly on top. Serve at once. Makes 6 servings.

Maritata

CREAMY NOODLE SOUP WITH CHEESE

Maritata, in Italian, means married; there is a fine blend or "marriage" of flavors in this elegant soup, yet it is delightfully easy to prepare. You cook a few strands of noodles in a rich broth—in a chafing dish at the table, if you like—then add a velvety mixture of sweet butter, cheese, egg yolks, and cream.

6	cups hot rich meat broth (all chicken, all beef, or combination of these, freshly made or canned)
2	ounces (⅛ of a 1-lb. package) vermicelli noodles
½	cup (¼ lb.) soft sweet (unsalted) butter
¾	cup freshly grated Parmesan cheese
4	egg yolks
1	cup heavy cream

Bring broth to boiling over direct heat (on a range top or over a denatured alcohol flame). Add vermicelli noodles (broken, if desired) and cook, uncovered, for 5 to 8 minutes or until noodles are tender to bite.

In a bowl blend the sweet butter with cheese and egg yolks, then gradually beat in the cream. (If you cook at the table, prepare this mixture in the kitchen.) Spoon a small amount of the hot broth into the cream mixture, stirring constantly, then pour this mixture back into the hot broth, stirring constantly. Extinguish heat, if using a chafing dish, or remove from the heat.

Ladle the soup into bowls, including some of the vermicelli. Makes 4 to 6 main-dish servings, 8 to 10 first-course servings.

GARNISH IDEAS FOR SOUPS

Often the difference between an everyday bowl of soup and one fit for company is the garnish. Even canned soups can be imaginatively presented and decorated.

Most soup garnishes are simple. Familiar crunchy garnishes are floating croutons, pretzels, and small crackers. Toasted, slivered nuts or a sprinkling of buttered, toasted crumbs may suit certain soups.

Sour cream and yogurt also are familiar additions, but don't forget a dollop of whipped cream or a pat of melting butter for much the same effect.

In clear soups such as consommé, a small bay leaf or spices such as peppercorns, a clove, or a piece of stick cinnamon lend interest and flavor.

Egg and cheese can provide color. The cheese may be grated and sprinkled on, or cubed. Hard-cooked egg whites or yolks may be sieved for sprinkling on, or the whites may be cut in thin strips.

Parsley, herbs, watercress, and mint are the most frequently used green garnishes. Float a tiny sprig or two of any which has compatible flavor, or mince very, very fine to sprinkle on the soup or even on top of another floating garnish. Green onion tops are attractive sliced in thin rings.

Paper-thin slices of lemon, lime, or orange to float or thin strips of peel give color, fragrance, and flavor. Floating citrus blossoms are also attractive.

Some bright-colored or crunchy vegetables may also be cut paper-thin—cucumber, carrots, radishes, beets, water chestnuts, and bamboo shoots.

Cold, jellied soups may be served in orange shells.

Carrot Soup

Carrots make a smooth and colorful cream soup. The flavor is subtle, a little different. A dusting of nutmeg seems just the right finish.

    4   pounds bony chicken pieces (backs, wings, necks)
    6   or 8 sprigs parsley
    10 or 12 carrots, peeled
    2   large onions, sliced
        About 2 teaspoons salt
    8   cups water
    1   cup heavy cream
        About ¼ teaspoon nutmeg

Tie chicken and parsley in a bag formed from a single thickness of cheesecloth. Place in a deep pot. Add carrots, onions, 1½ teaspoons of the salt, and the water. Cover, bring to a boil, and simmer slowly for 2 hours. Let cool slightly, then lift bag from broth and drain well. Discard bones and parsley.

Remove carrots and onions from broth with a slotted spoon and whirl in a blender with some of the broth in pan, stir in cream, ¼ teaspoon of the nutmeg, and additional salt if needed. (You can do this much a day ahead and chill soup, covered, overnight.) Heat to simmering. Ladle hot soup into bowls or mugs, and dust each serving lightly with nutmeg. Makes 10 to 12 servings of about 1 cup each.

Cream of Scallops

Bottled clam juice and scallops comprise this easy-to-make cream soup thickened with egg yolks, served hot. You can make the soup in just 5 to 10 minutes.

    2   bottles (8 oz. each) clam juice
    1   tablespoon butter or margarine
    ½   teaspoon each Worcestershire and dry mustard
    ⅛   teaspoon each garlic salt and celery salt
    ¾   pound scallops
    2   egg yolks
    1   cup heavy cream or half-and-half (light cream)
        Chopped parsley or chives

Heat clam juice, butter or margarine, Worcestershire, dry mustard, garlic salt, and celery salt in a pan. When just boiling, add cut-up scallops, and simmer gently about 3 minutes. Beat egg yolks with heavy cream or half-and-half; stir a little of the hot clam juice into the cream; then gradually stir the cream mixture into the remaining hot clam juice. Cook, stirring, about 1 minute, or just until liquid is slightly thickened. Garnish with chopped parsley or chives. Makes 4 servings.

Cream of Asparagus

In Mexico a cup or small bowl of a light but distinctly flavored soup is one of the most typical beginnings to a special meal. This Mexican soup, which contains cream cheese rather than cream in the sense you might expect, may be made with frozen asparagus.

    1   package (10 oz.) frozen cut asparagus
    4   cups chicken broth, canned or freshly made
        Salt
    2   small packages (3 oz. each) cream cheese or 1 cup sour cream

Combine the asparagus and broth in a saucepan and bring to boiling, uncovered. Stir to break apart asparagus and simmer gently, uncovered, for 10 minutes. Add salt to taste, if needed.

Cut the cream cheese into about ½-inch cubes and place in a soup tureen. Pour in the hot asparagus soup and serve at once. Or instead of using the cream cheese, you can pass sour cream to spoon into individual servings of the soup. Makes 6 to 8 servings.

Soupe de Légumes

PURÉE OF VEGETABLES

Travelers often bring back recipes for dishes they particularly liked while abroad, such as this French soup of six puréed vegetables.

    2   tablespoons butter or margarine
    1   large onion, chopped
    5   shallots or green onions, chopped
    2   leeks, sliced (include a little green top)
    2   cups cubed potatoes
    2   cups diced turnips
    1   medium-sized carrot, sliced
    1   medium-sized tomato, peeled and diced
    ½   teaspoon salt
    1   quart regular strength chicken broth or water
    3   tablespoons heavy cream
        Parsley or crisp croutons for garnish

Heat the butter in a large heavy pan, such as a Dutch oven. Add the onion, shallots or green onions, and leeks; sauté slowly, stirring, until the vegetables are golden, about 7 minutes. Add the potatoes, turnips, carrot, tomato, salt, and chicken broth or water; cover and simmer until all the vegetables are completely tender, about 20 minutes.

Whirl the soup, part at a time, in a blender until smooth. (Or put the soup through a food mill, or press through a wire strainer.) Add the cream to the puréed mixture, reheat, and serve each bowl garnished with a little fresh parsley or croutons. Makes 16 servings of ½ cup each.

Salad Tropical

This salad of whole fruits can be prepared so beautifully that it will double as centerpiece or buffet decoration. If you want to enjoy looking at it as long as possible, serve it for dessert—the sweet whipped cream dressing is just as suitable then.

> 1 each *large pineapple, large ripe pear, medium-sized or large papaya, and large ripe avocado*
> 1 can (1 lb. 4 oz.) *litchis, drained*
> *Lemon juice*
> 2 *large tangerines or 1 can (11 oz.) mandarin oranges, drained*
> 2 *large oranges*
> *Lettuce leaves*

Slice top, with leaves intact, from pineapple and save. Peel the fruit, cut in thick crosswise slices (do not core), and restack slices, finishing with the decorative top and leaves. Set pineapple on a serving tray. Arrange the following fruit around the pineapple in such a way as to retain the identity of each fruit: the unpeeled pear, cored and cut in wedges; the peeled and seeded papaya, cut in wide crosswise slices; the peeled and seeded avocado, cut in lengthwise slices; and the litchis. Brush pear and avocado with lemon juice.

Peel and section the tangerines, removing all white material, and group the pieces on the fruit platter (or use mandarins). Also peel the oranges with a knife, cut in crosswise slices, and place on the tray. Garnish with lettuce. Place a portion of each fruit on individual serving plates and top with the Cardamom Dressing. Makes 8 to 10 servings.

CARDAMOM DRESSING. Thoroughly beat 1 egg with 1½ tablespoons lemon juice, ⅛ teaspoon ground cardamom, and 1 tablespoon honey. Whip ½ cup heavy cream until stiff; add egg mixture, and continue to beat until mixture is softly whipped. Serve at once. Makes about 2 cups.

Green and Gold Salad

The bland green flavors of avocado and cucumber combine well with oranges and bananas, especially when topped with a piquant chutney dressing. Contrasts of texture and color make this salad pleasing.

> 1 *cucumber, thinly sliced*
> 1 can (11 oz.) *mandarin orange segments, well drained*
> 3 each *bananas and avocados, peeled and sliced*
> *Leaf lettuce*
> *Lemon juice*

Arrange cucumber and fruits on a large, lettuce-lined platter or eight individual salad plates. Brush bananas and avocados lightly with lemon juice if salad is to stand for a few minutes before serving. Drizzle about ½ cup of the Chutney Dressing over all. Garnish with cucumber and banana; serve with remaining dressing. Makes 8 servings.

CHUTNEY DRESSING. Place in blender container ½ cup *each* mayonnaise and sour cream, ⅓ cup chutney (including syrup), ¼ teaspoon curry powder, ½ teaspoon salt, ⅛ teaspoon liquid hot-pepper seasoning, 2 teaspoons salad oil, and 1 tablespoon white wine vinegar. Whirl until smooth. Makes 1⅓ cups.

Pico de Gallo

ORANGE AND VEGETABLE SALAD

This salad combines elements of a fresh relish served in the state of Jalisco, Mexico, which typically includes *jicama,* a mildly sweet root vegetable. If you can find it, add ½ to 1 cup, raw, peeled, and chopped, to this salad. In Mexico the relish is eaten with the fingers. Some imaginative person, perhaps an expert in shadow plays, decided the human hand picking up the tidbits looks like a rooster pecking corn; so the name *pico de gallo,* meaning "rooster's bill," was applied.

> 2 quarts *crisp, broken pieces of romaine*
> 1 *medium-sized orange, peeled and thinly sliced*
> ½ *cucumber, thinly sliced*
> ½ *sweet onion, slivered*
> ½ *green pepper, diced*
> ½ cup *salad oil or olive oil*
> ⅓ cup *wine vinegar*
> ½ teaspoon *salt*

Place romaine in a salad bowl. Arrange orange, cucumber, onion, and pepper on the greens. Garnish rim of the salad with tips of inner romaine leaves, if you wish.

Blend oil with vinegar and salt. Pour dressing over salad; mix lightly. Makes 8 servings.

Greens with Dilled Shrimp

Prepare everything for this salad, including the dill-marinated shrimp, ahead of time. All the ingredients can be cut or torn and refrigerated for tossing later.

¼	cup olive oil
1½	tablespoons white vinegar
1	tablespoon lemon juice
½	teaspoon dill weed
¼	teaspoon salt
⅛	teaspoon dry mustard
	Dash pepper
1	clove garlic, minced or mashed
½	pound cooked and shelled small shrimp
4	cups each chilled torn romaine and butter lettuce
¾	cup cubed Tilsit or jack cheese
½	cucumber, thinly sliced

Combine oil, vinegar, lemon juice, dill weed, salt, mustard, pepper, and garlic; shake well to blend. Pour over shrimp; cover and let stand for about 1 hour in refrigerator. To serve, mix shrimp mixture lightly with romaine, butter lettuce, cheese, and cucumber. Makes 6 servings.

Beefsteak Tomatoes and Onions

Men love this simple but delicious salad. For appearance and taste, choose the very best tomatoes—large, firm Beefsteaks only—and the sweetest red or Bermuda onions.

Oregano in the salad dressing provides the perfect simple seasoning.

2	large Beefsteak tomatoes
1	medium-sized Italian red or other mild sweet onion
¼	cup olive oil
2	teaspoons oregano
1	teaspoon salt

Cut tomatoes in ½-inch-thick slices; slice onion. Place in alternate layers in a large bowl. For the dressing, mix together olive oil, oregano, and salt. Pour the dressing over the tomatoes and onions, cover, and refrigerate for 1 hour or longer. Remove bowl from the refrigerator about 10 minutes before serving. Makes 6 servings.

DRESSING UP GREEN SALADS

Although a salad may consist of a single salad green, a variety of greens in the bowl can be more interesting. Start with a large quantity of a mild-flavored green, such as romaine or one of the lettuces (iceberg, leaf, Australian, or butter). Add a smaller quantity of the nippier greens. Among these are chicory (curly endive), escarole (broad leaf endive), watercress, spinach, young beet tops, dandelion, young mustard greens, Bok Choy (Chinese chard), and Chinese cabbage. Snip in a little of the pungent herbs and leaves—regular or Chinese parsley, other fresh herbs, mint, green onions including tops, chives, celery tops, the feathery part of fennel, or even peppery nasturtium leaves. For crispness you may add slices of celery, fennel stalk, leek, bulb onion, or Belgian endive.

If you want to add other more hearty and colorful ingredients to a salad, this list may serve as a reminder or idea stimulator: croutons, raw vegetables (tomato, cucumber, carrot, cauliflower, avocado, zucchini, shredded cabbage, sliced asparagus, radishes), cooked vegetables (many of the preceding plus peas, Chinese peas, beans, artichokes, potatoes, garbanzos, beets, bean sprouts, bamboo shoots, water chestnuts), cheese, hard-cooked eggs, mushrooms (raw or cooked), olives, salami, cold meats and fowl, shrimp, lobster, crab, tuna, anchovies, pickled peppers, pimiento, capers, pickle relish, and nuts. If you exercise discretion, you may also combine fruits with greens.

Oranges, tangerines, grapefruit, apple, grapes, banana, papaya, and pineapple are often used this way.

Following are some party dressings for your salad bowl:

French Dressing with Shallots. Blend together ¼ cup finely slivered shallots, 1 tablespoon prepared Dijon-style mustard, 6 tablespoons wine vinegar, ½ teaspoon salt, and ¾ cup salad oil or olive oil. Cover and keep as long as 2 days. (If you put dressing in the refrigerator, use safflower oil, because it stays clear and liquid.) Shake to blend again before serving. Makes about 1 cup.

Blue Cheese Dressing. Mix together 1 cup salad oil; 3 tablespoons red wine vinegar; 1 teaspoon salt; ¼ teaspoon *each* pepper and paprika; 1 clove garlic, minced; ½ teaspoon celery salt; and 1 tablespoon *each* lemon juice and Worcestershire. Gradually mix this into ½ cup (4 oz.) crumbled blue cheese. Chill, covered, for at least 8 hours to mellow flavors. Makes 1¾ cups dressing; allow 1 tablespoon dressing for each cup of salad greens.

Lime Salad Dressing. (Use on salads containing fruit.) Combine ½ cup *each* fresh lime juice and salad oil. Add 2 to 3 tablespoons honey, 1 teaspoon salt, 6 drops liquid hot-pepper seasoning, and ½ teaspoon ground ginger; shake or beat well before using. Makes enough for 8 to 10 servings.

Mixed Vegetables with Sweetbreads

The mild, smooth flavor of sweetbreads may have been appreciated in hot dishes; but it will be a taste experience for the adventuresome to have them cold, marinated in French dressing and tossed in a green salad. Anyone who does not care for sweetbreads may enjoy just the tossed greens.

- ½ cup salad oil
- 3 tablespoons white wine vinegar
- 2 teaspoons chopped parsley, chives, or basil
- ⅛ teaspoon each salt and dry mustard
- 1 pound sweetbreads, prepared as directed
- 3 cups mixed salad greens, washed, dried, and torn into pieces
- 2 tomatoes, peeled and cut in wedges
- ¼ cup each sliced celery and chopped green pepper

Combine the oil, vinegar, herbs, salt, and dry mustard and pour over the sweetbreads, prepared according to the following instructions. Cover and refrigerate several hours or overnight. Just before serving, drain the sweetbreads, and combine with the salad greens, tomatoes, celery, and green pepper. Dress the salad with the remaining marinade. Makes 6 servings.

PREPARING SWEETBREADS. Wash the sweetbreads well in cold water. Cover with cold water, and add 1 teaspoon salt and 1 tablespoon lemon juice per quart of water. Bring to a boil and simmer about 15 minutes. Drain and plunge the sweetbreads immediately into cold water for 5 minutes to cool them; drain.

With the point of a sharp knife (and your fingers), remove as much of the white connecting membranes as possible, breaking the sweetbreads into small, bite-sized pieces. If you are not going to use the sweetbreads immediately, place them in a glass bowl, cover with cool water, and refrigerate. Use within 24 to 36 hours.

Spinach with Pine Nut Dressing

To make this salad very special, buy the freshest spinach in quantity and select only the smallest leaves. You might experiment with lemon juice in place of vinegar in the dressing.

- ¾ cup toasted pine nuts, coarsely chopped
- ½ teaspoon tarragon
- ¼ teaspoon grated lemon peel
- ⅛ teaspoon nutmeg
- ½ cup salad oil or olive oil
- ⅓ cup vinegar
- ½ teaspoon salt
  Spinach leaves or half spinach and half butter lettuce
  Nutmeg

To toast nuts, spread them in a single layer on a pan; bake in a 350° oven for 5 minutes. Shake pan occasionally.

Blend nuts with tarragon, lemon peel, nutmeg, salad oil, vinegar, and salt. Mix well before using. Allow 2 tablespoons dressing for each cup of greens. Sprinkle each salad lightly with nutmeg to serve. Makes about 1⅔ cup dressing, enough for about 3 quarts torn greens. Makes 8 to 12 servings.

Green Peas in Sour Cream

Although this salad may look a bit unusual at first reading, it is amazingly delicious if you use very tiny peas and prepare them just as the recipe directs.

- 1 package (10 oz.) frozen small peas
- 1 tart, red-skinned apple
- 3 green onions, thinly sliced (include part of green tops)
- ½ cup sour cream
- ½ to 1 teaspoon prepared horseradish
- ¼ teaspoon salt
- ⅛ teaspoon pepper
- 2 teaspoons lemon juice
  Salad greens

Turn the peas from the package into a colander or wire strainer and run hot-test water from the tap over them just until thawed. Rinse in cold water, then drain thoroughly. (To hurry the draining, you might roll the peas on paper towels to absorb extra moisture.) Without peeling the apple, remove core and chop. Combine in a bowl the drained peas, chopped apple, and onion.

For the dressing, combine the sour cream, horseradish, salt, pepper, and lemon juice; add to the salad and mix together lightly. Serve in a bowl lined with crisp greens. Makes 4 to 6 servings.

Marinated Mushroom Salad

Plain tomato and lettuce gets dressed up with a topping of marinated raw mushrooms and onions. Since you can prepare the mushroom mixture well ahead of serving time, assembling the salad at the last minute is easy.

- ¼ to ½ pound fresh raw mushrooms
- 1 medium-sized sweet onion, thinly sliced
- ⅓ cup salad oil (may be half olive oil)
- ¼ cup tarragon wine vinegar
- 1 or 2 drops liquid hot-pepper seasoning
- ½ teaspoon salt
- 2 teaspoons minced parsley (fresh or freeze-dried)
- 1 medium-sized head iceberg lettuce
- 1 large tomato, peeled (optional)

Rinse mushrooms, pat dry, and slice lengthwise through the stems. Combine the mushrooms and the thinly sliced onions in the salad bowl. Over this pour the salad oil, wine vinegar, hot-pepper seasoning, salt, and parsley; mix gently.

Cover the bowl and let stand at room temperature for at least 4 hours.

Meanwhile wash the lettuce, drain well, wrap in a damp towel, and put into the refrigerator until well chilled and crisp.

Just before serving, break the lettuce into the bowl. If you use the tomato, cut it in wedges to add. Using a salad fork and spoon, mix all together lightly and well. Makes 6 servings.

Antipasto Potato Salad

This salad is so named because some of the ingredients are customarily part of Italian antipasto—salami, anchovies, and peppers. The potatoes are dressed with oil and vinegar rather than mayonnaise, as are most European potato salads; anise lightly flavors the dressing.

- 5 medium-sized potatoes (about 2 lbs.)
   Boiling salted water
- 1 green pepper, seeded and finely chopped
- ¼ cup each sliced green onion and finely chopped celery
- 6 thin slices Italian salami, cut in ½-inch strips (about ⅓ cup)
   Lettuce
- 2 hard-cooked eggs, cut in wedges
   Pickled red and green mild chiles (for garnish)

Scrub potatoes, and cook in their skins in boiling salted water until tender, about 40 minutes. Drain, peel as soon as possible, and cut into bite-sized ⅛-inch slices (you should have about 5½ cups). Place in bowl, and pour on Fennel Dressing. Cover and chill the potatoes for at least 2 hours, or as long as overnight.

Add green pepper, onion, celery, and salami; mix lightly. Cover and chill for about 1 hour longer. Serve in a lettuce-lined bowl, garnished with hard-cooked eggs and chiles. Makes 6 servings.

FENNEL DRESSING. Combine ⅓ cup salad oil, ¼ cup red wine vinegar, 1 clove garlic (minced or mashed), ¾ teaspoon *each* sugar and fennel seed or anise seed (crushed), ½ teaspoon *each* salt and basil, and a dash *each* pepper and cayenne. Beat until well combined. Drain 1 can (2 oz.) flat anchovy fillets, discarding the oil from the can; chop the anchovies and add to dressing.

Tomato Aspic with Vegetables

This dark red aspic is very rich with tomato and vegetable bits, including avocado.

You can turn it into an attractive entrée for luncheon by adding more cooked shrimp. Use a mayonnaise or sour cream dressing flavored with either lemon or horseradish.

- 3 envelopes unflavored gelatin
- ¾ cup cold water
- 2½ cups tomato juice
- 1 can (6 oz.) tomato paste
- ¼ cup vinegar
- 3 tablespoons lemon juice
- 1½ teaspoons basil
- 1 teaspoon each salt and sugar
- ⅛ teaspoon each onion powder and black pepper
- ½ teaspoon Worcestershire
- 1 cup chopped celery
- ½ cup chopped green pepper
- 1 avocado, diced
- 1 can (2¼ oz.) sliced ripe olives
   Cooked, chilled shrimp for garnish (optional)

Soften gelatin in the cold water. Bring 1 cup of the tomato juice to a boil; stir in the gelatin until dissolved. Add the remaining tomato juice, the tomato paste, vinegar, lemon juice, basil, salt, sugar, onion powder, black pepper, and Worcestershire. Refrigerate until partially thickened. Stir in the celery, green pepper, avocado, and olives. Pour into a 6-cup mold; refrigerate until set.

Unmold and garnish with shrimp, if you wish. Makes 6 to 8 servings.

Marinated Cauliflower

Cauliflower usually enters the salad picture raw. But in this recipe, flowerettes are very lightly cooked and marinated as long as overnight in a dressing redolent with essences of anchovies, capers, and olives.

    1   medium-sized cauliflower
         Boiling salted water
    ½   cup olive oil or other salad oil
    ¼   cup white vinegar
    ¾   teaspoon salt
    ¼   teaspoon each pepper and basil
    6   anchovy fillets, diced
    2   tablespoons capers
    ¼   cup sliced ripe olives
         Salad greens

Break cauliflower into flowerettes, wash, and drop into boiling, salted water. Cook for 7 minutes or so, until it is tender but still slightly crisp.

Drain, rinse in cold water, and drain again thoroughly. Put into a bowl. In another bowl or a glass jar, combine oil, vinegar, salt, pepper, and basil; shake or beat until well blended. Pour dressing over cauliflower. Add anchovy, capers, and olives; mix lightly. Cover and chill several hours or overnight, stirring several times.

To serve, lift the cauliflower with a slotted or runcible spoon, and arrange on the greens in the serving bowl. If you wish, serve the marinade as extra dressing to spoon over the salad. Makes 6 servings.

Swiss Cheese Salad

In Switzerland, diced cheese with vegetables and sharp dressing is often served as a first course. You will find other ways to use such a salad in American meals if you use it as you would potato or macaroni salad, which it most resembles.

    1   pound natural Swiss cheese, cut in
         ¼-inch cubes
    3   hard-cooked eggs, diced (reserve 1 yolk for
         garnish)
    ½   cup each chopped celery and chopped green
         pepper
    ½   cup mayonnaise
    1   tablespoon chopped chives
    2   teaspoons white wine vinegar
    1½   teaspoons prepared mustard
    ¼   teaspoon salt
         Lettuce leaves
         Cherry tomatoes for garnish

Mix together the cheese, eggs, celery, and green pepper. In another bowl, blend together the mayonnaise, chives, vinegar, mustard, and salt. Stir the dressing into the cheese mixture and refrigerate the salad until serving time.

To serve, mound the salad on individual lettuce leaves or in a bowl lined with the lettuce. Press reserved egg yolk through a fine wire strainer and sprinkle over salad. Use cherry tomatoes to garnish. (They add color, and the tomato-cheese flavor combination is delicious.) Makes 6 servings.

EVEN BUTTER CAN BE BEAUTIFUL

One of those special little touches that contributes to making entertaining special may be the butter you serve with your freshly baked breads—in fancy individual shapes on a bed of crushed ice. For shaping the butter, you will need to buy special utensils such as a cutter, curler, wooden paddles for making balls or "log" shapes, a "rose dish," which makes petal-shaped curls in the form of a blossom.

Butter Pat Cutter. The cutter, which resembles a wire egg slicer, cuts a stick of butter into restaurant-sized squares. Butter should be firm, and fresh from the refrigerator. Carefully place cutter on whole stick; press straight down, firmly. Put divided pats into ice water until you are ready to serve them.

Butter Curler. Pull curler, which looks much like a vegetable peeler, firmly across slightly softened butter; drop finished curls into ice water. Dip curler into hot water between curls. You can make several curls from each side of a stick of butter.

Wooden Paddles for Butter Balls or "Logs." You use two paddles which are scored to give the butter a textured finish. Use equal-sized chunks of slightly softened butter, and roll each into a ball between the paddles. Move paddles in tight circles, in opposite directions for ball, or back and forth for a log. Drop butter into ice water.

Silver Rose Dish for "Butter Blossom." Fill underside of dish with slightly softened butter. Set dish on its stand, press evenly to force the butter through patterned holes in dish; chill. Serve molded butter directly from dish.

To Make Sweet Butter. If you like sweet butter, yet consider it an extravagance or cannot find it to buy, make your own from ordinary salted butter. Cut the butter into chunks and cover it generously with ice water, then mix with an electric mixer or in a blender. Pour off and add fresh water at least twice, or until the salt is washed out. Drain, and knead or work with a spoon to remove the surplus water; then pack in jar, freeze until needed.

East Indies Cabbage Salad

Raw cabbage, of all the salad ingredients, can profit most from a pungent and imaginative dressing. Here many ingredients of Southeast Asian cooking are combined in a sweet-and-citrus dressing with peanut, soy sauce, and hot-pepper seasoning.

⅓	cup each *creamy peanut butter* and *sour cream*
1½	tablespoons *brown sugar*
1	teaspoon *curry powder*
2	tablespoons *lime or lemon juice*
1	tablespoon *soy sauce*
4	drops *liquid hot-pepper seasoning*
4	cups *finely shredded crisp cabbage*
½	cup each *sliced celery* and *sliced green onion*
	Salted peanuts or *pimiento*

For the dressing, combine the peanut butter, sour cream, brown sugar, curry powder, lime or lemon juice, soy sauce, and liquid hot-pepper seasoning in the container of your electric blender or in a bowl. Whirl or mix until the ingredients are well blended. This can be done ahead of time.

In a bowl combine the cabbage with the celery and green onions. Add dressing, and mix lightly. Garnish with a few salted peanuts or strips of pimiento, if you like. Serve immediately. Makes 6 servings.

Stuffed Avocado

Avocado meat has been removed from the shell, puréed, and mixed with seasoned gelatin. The smooth mixture is molded and served in the glossy green shell.

2	*avocados*
	Lemon juice
2	tablespoons *tarragon vinegar*
1	teaspoon each *salt* and *sugar*
	Dash *liquid hot-pepper seasoning*
2	tablespoons each *finely chopped chives, green pepper,* and *pimiento*
1	teaspoon *unflavored gelatin*
½	cup *cold water*
	Crisp greens for garnish
½	cup each *mayonnaise* and *sour cream*

Halve the avocados, discard seeds, and spoon out pulp, leaving about ¼ inch shell; brush inside each shell with lemon juice to prevent it from darkening. Combine avocado pulp in a blender with vinegar, salt, sugar, and hot-pepper seasoning; whirl until smooth (or mash together well). Stir in the chives, green pepper, and pimiento. Soften gelatin in water, then stir over hot water until dissolved. Stir gelatin into the avocado mixture. Chill until syrupy. Spoon

into avocado shells and chill until set.

Serve the salads on individual plates, with a garnish of crisp greens on each plate. Pass a dressing made by blending together the mayonnaise and sour cream. Makes 4 servings.

Snow Peas with Sesame Dressing

Those crisp green pea pods, so good in hot Chinese dishes, make a great salad, too. This one also contains cauliflower and water chestnuts, often combined with the peas in stir-fry Chinese dishes. Toasted sesame seed contribute color and crunch. Now that Chinese peas are available frozen, the salad can be enjoyed anytime, everywhere.

1	package (7 oz.) *frozen Chinese (edible pod) peas*
	Boiling salted water
½	head *cauliflower*
1	can (5 oz.) *water chestnuts,* drained and sliced
1	tablespoon *chopped pimiento*

Cook Chinese peas in a small amount of boiling salted water until barely tender, about 1 minute after water boils; drain. Separate cauliflower into bite-sized clusters (you should have about 2 cups); cook in boiling salted water until tender but still crisp, about 3 minutes after water boils; drain. Combine peas and cauliflower with water chestnuts and pimiento; cover and chill. Just before serving, mix with about 3 tablespoons Sesame Seed Dressing. Makes 4 to 6 servings.

SESAME SEED DRESSING. Place 2 tablespoons sesame seed in a shallow pan in a 350° oven for 5 to 8 minutes or until golden brown; cool. In jar with a lid combine ⅓ cup salad oil; 1 tablespoon *each* lemon juice, vinegar, and sugar; ½ clove garlic, minced and mashed; ½ teaspoon salt; and toasted sesame seed. Cover and chill. Shake well before using.

Distinctive Entrées

THE ENTRÉE IS THE MOST IMPORTANT PART of a meal, and the deciding factor in all the other things you serve before, with, or after.

The foremost consideration in the selection of these entrées has been whether they are practical for entertaining. Nearly all of these dishes may be made partially or entirely ahead; many may be frozen. Many use convenience foods or shortcuts to simplify the preparation.

In addition to the usual dishes considered to be entrées, salads and soups substantial enough for a main dish are included. These have always been popular lunch dishes, but are increasingly served for evening meals, particularly informal or late suppers.

Recipes range from very simple to complex production numbers, but all are distinguished by being particularly delicious or interesting. There should be something just right for any occasion you plan, informal or elegant, in any season and at any time of day.

Beef Burgundy

This entrée is a simple version of the traditional French Boeuf Bourguignonne. Lean chunks of beef are combined with pearl onions, fresh mushrooms, Burgundy, and seasonings. You can flame the meat with brandy if you wish. Beef Burgundy goes especially well with a wild rice casserole.

16	small white onions, peeled (about 1 pound)
6	slices lean bacon, diced
¼	cup (⅛ lb.) butter or margarine
4	pounds beef chuck, cut in 1½-inch cubes, fat trimmed off
¼	cup brandy (optional)
1½	teaspoons salt
¼	teaspoon freshly ground pepper
2	cups Burgundy or other dry red wine
2	whole cloves garlic, peeled
2	cups small fresh mushrooms, whole or sliced
1½	cups water
	Bouquet Garni: Tie in a piece of cheesecloth 1 or 2 sprigs parsley, 1 celery top, 1 quartered carrot, a bay leaf, and a sprig of thyme (or 1 teaspoon dried thyme)
6	tablespoons flour
½	cup cold water

Brown onions with bacon and butter in a Dutch oven; remove onions and bacon with a slotted spoon, and reserve.

Add the meat to the pan and brown well on all sides. If desired, pour brandy over the beef and set aflame, tilting the pan to keep the flame going as long as possible. Sprinkle the meat with the salt and pepper.

Add Burgundy, garlic, mushrooms, the 1½ cups water, bouquet garni, onions, and bacon. Cover and simmer approximately 1½ hours, or until the meat is tender.

Lift the beef, mushrooms, and onions out of the pan with a slotted spoon; arrange in a covered 3-quart casserole or baking dish, or in a serving dish if you plan to serve at once.

Strain the liquid through a sieve, discarding the bouquet garni, garlic, and bacon. Mix the flour to a smooth paste with the ½ cup cold water; stir into the meat stock and cook, stirring, until the gravy is thick and smooth.

Pour gravy over the meat and serve immediately, or refrigerate and reheat, covered, in a 350° oven for about 35 minutes, or until hot and bubbly. Serve over rice or with a wild rice casserole, if you wish. Makes 8 servings.

Pozharsky

The word *pozharsky* comes from the Russian *pozhar*, meaning "fire"—referring to the final flaming of the dish with brandy.

        About ¾ cup butter or margarine
1   large potato, peeled and thinly sliced
1   pound boneless tender lean beef or veal,
            cut about ½ inch thick
1   large onion, sliced
¼   pound mushrooms, sliced (about 1½ cups)
4   whole slices eggplant, ⅜ inch thick
1   large tomato, peeled
1   package (9 oz.) frozen asparagus spears
        Boiling salted water
1½   tablespoons flour
1   cup beef broth
½   cup dry white wine
1   tablespoon each tomato paste and lemon juice
¼   teaspoon each salt, basil, and dry mustard
        Dash pepper
3   tablespoons brandy

Heat 2 tablespoons of the butter in a large frying pan over medium heat. Cook potatoes, lifting and turning them often, just until tender and slightly browned. Arrange potatoes over bottom of a shallow 1½-quart casserole or 4 individual baking dishes. Add 2 tablespoons more butter to frying pan; brown meat quickly on all sides over high heat. Cook meat to preferred doneness and arrange over potatoes.

Add 1 tablespoon of the butter to the same pan and sauté onions; spoon over meat. Then sauté mushrooms in about 2 more tablespoons of the butter or margarine, cooking until liquid from the mushrooms has evaporated; spoon over onion. Add 3 tablespoons of the butter to the pan and cook eggplant slices until tender and lightly browned on both sides. Arrange slices over vegetables in casserole.

Slice tomato in four thick slices and place on top of eggplant slices. Cook asparagus in boiling salted water just until tender; drain and arrange over tomato slices or around the side of the dish.

To make sauce, heat the remaining 1½ tablespoons butter or margarine in a pan and stir in flour; cook about 1 minute, browning lightly. Gradually add beef broth and wine, and cook, stirring, until sauce is smooth and slightly thickened. Stir in tomato paste, lemon juice, salt, basil, dry mustard, and pepper. Spoon sauce evenly over vegetables. (At this point, you can cover and refrigerate the dish.)

Bake, covered, in a 350° oven for about 40 minutes for a large casserole or 25 minutes for individual dishes; sauce should be bubbly and vegetables and meat well heated. (If you refrigerate the dish before baking, increase baking time about 20 minutes.) Just before serving, warm the brandy, ignite, and pour flaming over the casserole (or casseroles). Makes 4 servings.

Stuffed Grape Leaves or Cabbage

For centuries many Mediterranean countries have used grape leaves to enhance the flavor of different foods. Stuffed grape leaves, called *dolmathes* in Greek, are prepared with a variety of fillings and served as appetizer or main course. Grape leaves, packed in bottles, can be found in many specialty food stores. Cabbage leaves are also used for dolmathes, sometimes called dolma, in various Near and Middle Eastern countries.

1   pound lean ground beef
1   large onion, chopped
½   cup uncooked rice
3   tablespoons butter or margarine
½   cup chopped parsley
¼   cup chopped mint
2   teaspoons salt
1   teaspoon each pepper and dill weed
3   or 4 dozen canned grape leaves or 1 medium
            head cabbage
1   cup water

Combine ground beef, onion, rice, butter, parsley, mint, salt, pepper, and dill. Wash grape leaves in hot water; drain on paper toweling (To use cabbage leaves instead, see instructions at end of recipe.)

Spread 1 grape leaf on a flat surface with the underside up and the stem end toward you; cut off the stem. Place about 2 teaspoons of filling near the stem end, then fold the sides of the leaf over the filling and roll away from you. Continue until all the filling is used. Do not roll tightly, as the rice will expand when it cooks.

Place close together in a large kettle (at least 6-quart size) on a layer of grape leaves. Add water and place a heatproof plate on top of rolls to prevent them from breaking apart. Cover pan and simmer for 40 minutes, or until rice is tender. Drain rolls, saving the cooking liquid. Serve with Avgolemono Sauce. Makes about 40 rolls, or 8 to 10 servings.

AVGOLEMONO SAUCE. Beat 3 eggs until foamy and add 3 tablespoons lemon juice, 1 tablespoon at a time. Strain the cooking liquid from the dolmathes into a saucepan and heat. Pour a little of the hot liquid into the egg mixture, stirring with a fork. Gradually pour this into the hot liquid in the pan. Cook over low heat, stirring constantly, just until thickened. Do not boil or egg will separate.

Note: To use cabbage in place of grape leaves, separate the leaves from the head of cabbage and place in boiling water, letting them stand until they are quite pliable. Remove from water and trim away the thick stem. Place about 1 tablespoon of filling near the center of each leaf; fold sides of leaf over filling and roll.

STEAK—A FAVORITE PARTY ENTRÉE

The variety in names, sizes, and shapes of steaks understandably causes much confusion. To simplify this complex situation as much as possible, a division into three types helps—steaks from the loin, those from the rib, and those from other parts of the steer.

Steaks from the Loin. These are named according to the part of the loin from which they are cut. Club steaks are from the small end of the loin. Next cuts (and next in size) are the T-bones, then the porterhouse steaks (on one side of the bone is the fillet and the other the New York or strip, often cut and sold separately). Last and largest in size are the sirloins, which often are cut apart into three steaks—fillet, top sirloin, and culotte. The fillet muscle (also called filet mignon and tenderloin) runs from T-bone through sirloin sections and can, of course, be cut out in a whole long strip. When cut extra-thick for two persons, a fillet steak is called Châteaubriand.

Steaks from the Rib. Slices of the entire section containing rib bone, tender rib eye, and less tender top muscles are sold as rib steaks. When the choice central muscle or "eye" is cut out and sold alone, this is called a rib eye, market, or spencer steak. Some experts consider rib steaks the most flavorful of all, because of their generous streaking of fat.

Steaks from Other Parts of the Steer. These mostly are from the round and shoulder or chuck, and certain other muscles that are tender enough to broil or barbecue. The skirt steak, for instance, is from inside the rib cage and only two are on each animal.

All these steaks are less tender than loin, but they vary considerably in tenderness. Most of them need or at least profit by tenderizing with vinegar, wine, citrus juice, commercial powdered meat tenderizer, or some flavorful marinade. These steaks are most tender when done fairly rare; they become less tender when medium or well done.

A full round steak may be cut and sold in three different parts—top round (the most tender), bottom round (Swiss steak), and eye of round. Bottom and eye of round should be tenderized before broiling or barbecueing.

Center-cut cross rib steaks are the sliced center portions of a cross-rib chuck roast and are tender enough that marinating is optional.

Two other kinds of steaks come from the chuck—the blade-bone chuck and 7-bone chuck. These steaks should be cut about 1½ inches thick, cooked rare, and thinly sliced. Tenderize if you wish.

The skirt steak is a thin strip of meat, usually purchased rolled into a pinwheel and fastened with a wooden skewer. Tenderizing may improve these steaks, but is not necessary.

Lean flank steak, with coarse fibers, is at its best if scored before cooking, broiled rare, and sliced diagonally.

Another cut, the hanging tenderloin (there's only one to a steer), also benefits from the same treatment as flank steak; marinating enhances its flavor.

The sirloin tip, cut from between the sirloin and the round, is best cut an inch thick and tenderized.

BAKE-BROIL METHOD FOR COOKING STEAKS

When you broil or barbecue a very thick steak, it's a bit tricky to make sure it's done to just the right degree—well browned on the outside, pink within.

This combination bake-broil method assures a medium-rare result. You begin by placing a 2-inch-thick steak in a very slow oven for 2 hours or more, then broil or barbecue it just long enough to brown the outside. Steaks prepared this way remain juicy and shrink little. There is also little spattering of fat.

This method is well suited to entertaining, for it enables you to time the serving of the steak precisely. Carve the steak as you would a roast, cutting in vertical ⅜ to ½-inch-thick slices.

For Tender Steaks (Such as Porterhouse, Sirloin, Rib). Stand a 2-inch-thick steak on edge in a V-shaped rack in a roasting pan. Place in a 200° oven for 2 hours. Then place flat on a rack and broil or grill on each side until well browned (3 to 5 minutes for each side). Season with salt and pepper.

For Less-Tender Steaks (Such as Chuck, Sirloin Tip, Round). Prepare meat by brushing lightly with water on each side; sprinkle each side with unseasoned meat tenderizer (allow a total of ½ teaspoon tenderizer per pound of meat), then pierce with a fork at ½-inch intervals. Stand steak on edge in a V-shaped rack in a roasting pan. Place in a 200° oven allowing 45 minutes per pound of meat. Then place flat on a rack and broil or grill on each side until well browned (3 to 5 minutes per side). Season with salt and pepper.

AN ALL-PURPOSE STEAK SAUCE

The following classic steak sauce is delicious with any kind of steak.

Blender Béarnaise. Simmer 3 tablespoons white wine vinegar with 1 teaspoon *each* tarragon (crumbled) and chopped chives or green onions until reduced to about 2 teaspoons. Place in a blender container with 2 whole eggs and 2 tablespoons lemon juice. Blend a few seconds; then, with blender turned on, slowly pour in 1 cup hot melted butter. Turn into a sauce bowl. (If made ahead, reheat over a pan of hot tap water.) Makes 1½ cups.

Steak, Mushrooms, and Asparagus

Serve this quickly prepared beef, mushroom, and asparagus dish with an oil and vinegar-dressed salad, buttered brown rice, hard French rolls, and red wine.

    1¼   pounds flank steak
    ½   pound mushrooms, sliced (about 3 cups)
    2   cups asparagus (about 1 pound fresh) cut
            in ½-inch diagonal slices
          Water
    1   tablespoon cornstarch
    ¼   cup dry red wine
    1   teaspoon salt
    ½   teaspoon thyme
    ¼   teaspoon each tarragon and garlic powder
    3   tablespoons olive oil

Cut flank steak in half lengthwise; slice each half, on the diagonal, into ¼-inch-thick strips. Place vegetables in a large, heavy frying pan that has a cover. Add 1 cup water. Cover, bring to a boil, and cook over medium-high heat for about 5 minutes or until asparagus is barely tender. Drain, reserving liquid, and place in an uncovered bowl.

Add ½ cup water to cornstarch gradually, blending until smooth; mix in wine, salt, thyme, tarragon, and garlic powder. Brown meat quickly in very hot olive oil; reduce heat, return vegetables to pan with cornstarch mixture, and cook for about 1 minute longer, stirring constantly, until sauce is thickened. Blend in about ⅓ cup of the reserved vegetable liquid if you prefer a thinner sauce. Makes 4 servings.

Giant Beef-Lobster Kebabs

Meat for six people cooks on just two long skewers for these kebabs. If you use round steak, it might be wise to prepare it with instant meat tenderizer, following the directions on the container.

    1½   to 2 pounds top sirloin or top round steak,
            cut in 2-inch cubes
    3   frozen lobster tails (about 1½ pounds), split
            lengthwise and thawed
    ⅓   cup each dry white wine and salad oil
    1   tablespoon lemon juice
          Lemon wedges

Thread skewers alternating beef cubes with lobster. An attractive way to do this is to wrap the lobster tail around a piece of beef and thread the skewer through the thick end of lobster tail, the beef cube, then the other end of the lobster tail. You can put three of these combinations onto each long skewer. Grill over hot coals for 8 to 12 minutes, or until lobster flakes and beef is done to your liking. Baste while cooking with a mixture of the wine, salad oil, and lemon juice. Serve hot with lemon wedges and Tomato Béarnaise sauce.

TOMATO BÉARNAISE. Combine in blender 3 egg yolks and 1½ tablespoons tarragon vinegar. Melt ¾ cup butter, turn blender on high speed and immediately pour in the hot butter in a steady stream. Add ½ teaspoon salt, ½ teaspoon tarragon, and 3 tablespoons finely chopped parsley; whirl until blended, about 30 seconds. Mix in 2 tablespoons tomato purée. Makes about 2 cups sauce.

Veal Veronique

WITH GRAPES IN WINE

Green seedless grapes, often paired with delicate fish in French cuisine, are used here with mild veal simmered in white wine. The dish has a sumptuous look that belies the fact it is a dieter's delight.

    1   pound boneless veal round, cut about ⅓ inch
            thick
    2   tablespoons flour
    ½   teaspoon salt
    ⅛   teaspoon pepper
    2   tablespoons salad oil
    ½   cup dry white wine
    ¼   teaspoon grated lemon peel
    ¼   teaspoon rosemary, crumbled
    ½   pound seedless grapes, separated into small
            clusters

Cut the veal into serving-sized pieces. Combine flour, salt, and pepper; gently pound into the veal. Heat the oil in a frying pan; brown meat on both sides. Add wine; sprinkle with lemon peel and rosemary. Cover and simmer slowly for about 15 minutes. Add the grapes, cover again, and continue cooking 5 minutes longer or until tender. Makes 4 servings.

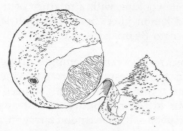

Veal Roast Orloff

This roast makes a dramatic appearance, yet is simple to do. You first roast a plain veal sirloin tip, then cut the meat into slices (handy for serving later). Between slices you insert Canadian bacon and Gruyère cheese. You also spread creamy onion sauce between the slices and over the top. The roast goes back in the oven long enough to heat meat, melt the cheese, and brown the sauce. Everything except the final heating and browning can be done as much as a day ahead.

3 to 4-pound veal sirloin tip roast
   Salt
   Pepper
   Soubise Sauce (recipe follows)
½ pound sliced, fully cooked Canadian bacon
   About 6 ounces natural Gruyère cheese
2 tablespoons shredded Gruyère

Sprinkle roast with salt and pepper. Place, fat-side up, on a rack in a shallow pan. Roast in a 325° oven for about 2¼ hours to a temperature of 160° on a meat thermometer. Remove from oven and let rest 15 minutes. Remove strings.

Cutting to within ½ inch of bottom, cut veal into ½-inch slices. Spread 1 cut side of each slice generously with Soubise Sauce (recipe follows), reserving half for topping. Insert a thin slice of Canadian bacon next to sauce on each slice, then insert 1 thin slice Gruyère cheese between bacon and each of the unspread surfaces of veal. Tie a string around roast to hold it together. Spread remaining sauce over the top; sprinkle with shredded Gruyère. If making ahead, cover loosely and chill.

Return to 325° oven; bake about 45 minutes, or until meat is heated through and sauce is lightly browned. Cut between slices to serve. Makes 10 to 12 servings.

SOUBISE SAUCE. Cook 1 cup chopped onion in 2 tablespoons butter until soft. Use blender or food mill to purée; return to pan. Blend ½ cup flour, ½ teaspoon salt, ¼ teaspoon nutmeg, and a dash pepper; stir into onion purée and cook about 2 minutes. Gradually add ½ cup *each* chicken broth and heavy cream. Cook, stirring constantly, until sauce is thick. Beat 1 egg yolk; blend in a little of the hot sauce. Blend into remaining sauce and cook, stirring, until smooth and thick.

Stuffed Smoked Pork Chops

Smoked pork is quite similar to ham in flavor. The chops are particularly good stuffed; have your meatman cut a pocket in each for stuffing. Although simple to prepare, this dish is special enough for a party.

1 cup cooked rice
¼ cup each chopped raisins and chopped
      green pepper
1 tablespoon each vinegar and chopped
      pimiento
¼ teaspoon oregano
6 slices bacon, cooked, drained, crumbled
6 thick smoked pork chops, cut with pocket
      for stuffing
2 tablespoons butter or salad oil
½ cup water

Mix together the rice, raisins, green pepper, vinegar, pimiento, oregano, and bacon. Stuff each chop (do not pack); close with short skewers or wooden picks and lace with string. Brown chops on both sides in the butter or oil; add the water, cover, and simmer about 30 minutes, or until tender. Makes 6 servings.

Pork Loin with Sautéed Papaya

At the self-service meat counter, most pork loins have been partially cut into individual chops for easier carving at a guest meal. You can ask to have the roast cut this way if it's not already done.

4 pound pork loin roast
⅓ cup each catsup and orange juice
1 teaspoon grated orange peel
½ teaspoon ground ginger
1 papaya
2 tablespoons butter
   Juice of ½ lime
3 to 4 cups hot cooked rice
   Parsley

Place roast on a rack in a shallow roasting pan; insert meat thermometer into thickest part. Combine catsup, orange juice, grated orange peel, and ginger; brush part of this sauce over meat. Roast, uncovered, in a 325° oven until meat thermometer registers 170°. Baste several times with remaining sauce.

Just before serving, peel papaya, halve, and scoop out seeds. Slice papaya and sauté slices in butter; turn to brown all sides lightly. Squeeze lime juice over papaya in pan. Spoon hot cooked rice onto a warm serving platter. Place roast or slices of roast on rice; arrange papaya slices around meat and pour any butter remaining in the pan over the fruit. Garnish with parsley, if you wish. Makes 8 servings.

Baked Ham with Jewel Fruit Sauce

This receipe is a jewel of a find for the hostess whose husband balks at carving meat. The ham is presliced and tied by the meatman. The slices are skewered through the middle to hold them together after baking. At serving time, the skewer is gradually pulled out to release the slices of ham one by one as they are needed. You should estimate about ⅓ pound of ham per serving.

> 7 to 12-pound canned ham
> Jewel Fruit Sauce (recipe follows)

Have your meatman slice and tie a flat-topped canned ham. Bake according to directions on can or in a 325° oven until meat is heated. Prepare Jewel Fruit Sauce (recipe follows).

About 20 minutes before meat is done, drain off all pan juices. Pour the ½ cup fruit sauce you reserved for glazing over the ham; bake 20 minutes more. Pour rest of sauce, including fruit, over ham; bake until fruit is heated.

Place the ham on a serving platter. Insert 1 or 2 skewers through the slices and remove the string. Arrange the fruits over the ham. Serve the remaining sauce separately.

JEWEL FRUIT SAUCE. Drain 1 can (1 lb. 14 oz.) fruits for salad (or 3½ cups canned fruits, a combination of your favorites), saving ½ cup syrup. (If you use several kinds of fruits, combine the juices and then measure.)

Blend 1 tablespoon cornstarch with a small amount of reserved syrup, 1 cup apple juice or cider, 3 or 4 tablespoons brown sugar, 1 tablespoon soy sauce, 1 teaspoon dry mustard, 2 tablespoons lemon juice, ½ teaspoon grated lemon peel, and 2 or 3 tablespoons of pan juices from the ham.

Bring to a boil, stirring, and cook until clear and slightly thickened. Remove from heat; set aside ½ cup sauce for glazing ham. Add drained fruit to the rest of the sauce.

GARNISHING THE ENTRÉE

Have you ever noticed how glamorous even an ordinary dish seems in fine restaurants? Often it's the garnish that does it.

Elegant garnishes may take time, but they are a nice touch when you're entertaining.

Easy Garnish Ideas. A sautéed fish or broiled steak takes especially well to decorating; lay 3 or 4 ribbons of smoked salmon or anchovy fillets over the top, pour on melted butter, and add a wedge of lemon or sprig of fresh dill or watercress.

To garnish meat platters, fill artichoke bottoms (canned, if you wish) with tiny shrimp or sliced mushrooms cooked in butter. Large cooked mushroom caps may be filled with such tidbits as chicken livers, chopped ham, or sautéed onions. Cooked whole turnips, onions, or tomatoes can also be formed into cups to stuff with a rice or vegetable mixture or with butter-browned mushrooms.

Any meat platter or roast can be beautified with small fresh, cooked, or preserved fruits such as crab apples, kumquats, cranberries, cherries, grape bunches, or pineapple spears.

Cherry tomatoes, radish roses, scored mushroom caps (either raw or sautéed in butter), and toast points are other simple garnishes in addition to the frequently used sprigs or beds of watercress and parsley.

Citrus slices or wedges can be beautified with a sprinkling of finely minced parsley or paprika. A clove or parsley sprig stuck in the center of a slice is another variation.

Sliced rounds may be twisted into an interesting "S" shape (cut the round half way through to the center, then twist one of the cut sides to the left and the other to the right; stand up with the twisted points as bases).

Fruit Brochettes. To garnish a meat platter, thread small fruits or pieces of fruit on slender bamboo skewers. Use any fruit combination you like—pineapple chunks, banana slices, spiced figs or peaches, grapes, maraschino cherries. Coat fruits with lime juice and maple syrup, or with melted butter and a light sprinkling of curry powder. Just before serving, heat through under broiler or bake in a 450° oven just until hot.

Cranberry Jelly Slices. To ring a meat platter or top a casserole, slice cranberry jelly about ¼ inch thick and cut into interesting shapes with cooky cutters. Center on large orange slices or pineapple rings.

Brandied Peaches. Garnish platter with brandied peaches decorated with cinnamon stick stems and leaves cut from citron.

Citrus Cups. A serving platter of fish can be enhanced by individual lime or lemon cups brimming with tartar sauce. Slice off pointed ends of fruit halves to make a flat bottom. Ream, and score or scallop the cut rim of the cups, if you wish. Fill with sauce. (Seeded pepper halves could also be used.)

Layered Ham Pancakes

RAKOTT SONKÁS PALACSINTA

Palacsinta (pal-a-*chin*-ta) is a thin Hungarian pancake that is not much different from the better-known French pancake, or crêpe, except that it is even more thin and eggy.

The French use crêpes in many ways, but Hungarian cooks have gone even further with palacsinta. They roll them, fold them, cut them, and stack them. They fill and embellish them with all sorts of savory and sweet mixtures. They use the pancakes as entrées, in soups, and for fancy desserts—but never for breakfast.

This "stack" of pancakes with minced ham filling is one of their most delicious entrée creations. It is a good idea to make Hungarian pancakes ahead of time and assemble them just in time to heat and serve. If you want to make the pancakes more than a day ahead, just freeze the cooled and stacked pancakes; allow to thaw completely before you begin to work with them.

> Hungarian Pancakes (recipe follows)
> 2 cups ground cooked smoked ham
> 1 cup sour cream
> 2 tablespoons finely minced green onions
> ¼ teaspoon salt
> ⅛ teaspoon Dijon-style mustard (or other prepared hot mustard)
> Dash of pepper
> About 1 tablespoon butter
> Sour cream

You'll need about 12 Hungarian Pancakes (one basic recipe below). For the filling, combine ham, 1 cup sour cream, green onions, salt, mustard, and a dash of pepper. Place one of the pancakes on a buttered baking dish or heatproof plate; spread with a thin layer of the ham filling. Repeat, using all the filling and pancakes, ending with a pancake on top. Dot the top with about 1 tablespoon butter.

Bake in a 350° oven for about 20 minutes or until heated through. Garnish with spoonfuls of sour cream just before serving. Cut in wedges to serve. Makes 4 servings.

HUNGARIAN PANCAKES (PALACSINTA). Beat 3 eggs with a fork. Add 6 tablespoons unsifted flour and ⅜ teaspoon salt; continue beating until batter is smooth. Gradually add 1 cup milk, beating again until smooth. Using an 8-inch crêpe pan or frying pan, heat about 3 tablespoons butter (½ to 1 tablespoon for each pancake) over medium-high heat until bubbly. Pour in about 3 tablespoons batter (all at once) for each pancake; quickly tilt and rotate pan so the batter completely covers the bottom of the pan. When lightly brown on bottom, turn with long, flexible spatula and lightly brown on other side.

Ham and Bananas

This dish is so quick to prepare that you might keep it in mind for those emergency times when guests drop in. You can also dress up the rice pilaf in a number of ways, depending on what ingredients you have on hand.

> 2 tablespoons butter or margarine
> 2 tablespoons honey
> 2 tablespoons Sherry or apple juice
> 1 teaspoon lemon juice
> ⅛ teaspoon nutmeg
> Dash of ground cloves
> 1 center-cut ham slice, about 1 inch thick (1½ to 2 lbs.)
> 2 firm, ripe bananas
> Rice
> Raisins
> Dash of nutmeg

Combine in a small pan the butter or margarine, honey, Sherry or apple juice, lemon juice, nutmeg, and dash of ground cloves. Heat until butter is melted. Put ham slice in preheated broiler about 4 inches below heat; broil 5 minutes, or until browned.

Meanwhile peel bananas and slice in half, lengthwise. Turn over ham slice, arrange half-slices of banana on top, then brush the butter-honey mixture all over top of ham and bananas. Put back under broiler and broil about 5 minutes more, or until browned, basting several times with the remaining butter-honey mixture. Serve the banana-topped ham on a bed of hot rice pilaf—add a handful of raisins and a dash of nutmeg to rice while it is cooking. Makes 4 servings.

Braculine

STUFFED PORK ROLLS

These Italian rolls of pork are filled with a most unusual, flavorful stuffing of pine nuts, prosciutto (the salty Italian ham), and mashed hard-cooked eggs. The rolls are browned, then simmered in tomato sauce. Serve them with toasted pine nuts sprinkled on top and lemon wedges—a little lemon juice is just the right piquant finish.

> 1½ cups and 2 tablespoons pine nuts
> ⅛ pound (2 oz.) prosciutto, minced
> ¼ cup minced parsley
> ¼ teaspoon marjoram
> 2 hard-cooked eggs, mashed fine
> 2 pounds pork tenderloin
> 2 tablespoons butter
> ½ cup each canned tomato sauce and water
> Lemon wedges

To toast nuts, spread them in single layer in pan; bake in a 350° oven 5 minutes. Shake occasionally. Finely chop all but the 2 tablespoons nuts with a knife, or whirl a few at a time in a blender. Blend well with prosciutto, parsley, marjoram, and eggs, mashing together so mixture is slightly compacted. Set aside while you prepare meat.

Trim excess fat from tenderloin and discard; cut meat in 12 equal-size pieces. Place each portion of meat between sheets of waxed paper and pound very thin with a flat-surfaced mallet; the meat will tear apart easily but should have no holes. Divide filling evenly among pounded meat pieces and pat over surface. Roll to enclose filling and hold shut with small wooden skewers. (You can do this several hours ahead and keep cold, covered.)

Melt butter in a wide frying pan over moderate heat and lightly brown the filled rolls on all sides. Take care not to brown excessively as this hardens meat and makes it dry. Then add tomato sauce and water to pan, cover, and simmer over low heat for 12 to 15 minutes, turning rolls occasionally. Remove rolls to a serving dish and pour the pan juices over the meat. Sprinkle with the reserved 2 tablespoons pine nuts. Squeeze a little lemon on each serving. Makes 6 servings.

Provençal Lamb Shoulder

Stuffed with a mixture of pork and olives, this boneless lamb roast is easy to carve. Because of the pork inside, it should be cooked to a temperature of 170° on the meat thermometer.

½   pound ground pork
1   clove garlic, minced or mashed
¼   cup finely chopped onion
½   cup sliced pimiento-stuffed green olives
¼   teaspoon each salt and whole thyme
    Dash pepper
1   egg
3   slices whole wheat bread
2   tablespoons milk
3   pound boned lamb shoulder roast
    Olive oil

Lightly mix pork, garlic, chopped onion, olives, salt, thyme, pepper, egg (slightly beaten), bread (with the crusts trimmed and bread cut in ½-inch cubes), and milk.

Fill cavity in roast with this mixture; sew edges closed with string or heavy thread. Rub olive oil lightly over surface of meat. Place stuffed roast on rack in an uncovered roasting pan in a 325° oven for about 2¼ hours or until meat thermometer inserted in thickest part registers 170°. Remove strings; place meat on a warm platter. If you like, you may skim and thicken pan drippings to make a sauce. Makes 6 servings.

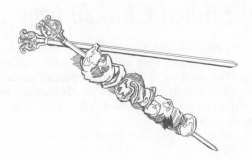

Mustard-Coated Lamb Roll

French mustard coats this boneless roast from a leg of lamb. If you have never tried lamb cooked medium rare rather than well done, try this roast that way—the meat is much more juicy and tender.

4½ to 5-pound boned, rolled leg of lamb
⅓   cup Dijon-style mustard
1   tablespoon soy sauce
¼   teaspoon each garlic salt and ground ginger
1   teaspoon dried rosemary (crumbled)
1   tablespoon salad oil

Place meat on a rack on a roasting pan. For coating, mix together mustard, soy sauce, garlic salt, ground ginger, rosemary, and salad oil.

Spread over roast, coating completely, and let stand at least 1 hour. Insert a meat thermometer and roast in a 300° oven until the thermometer registers 150° for pinkish rare meat (about 1½ hours) or 160° for medium well done. Remove to a platter and carve. Makes 10 to 12 servings.

Arni Souvlakia

GREEK-STYLE SHISH KEBAB

You might alternate these lamb cubes on the skewers with small tomatoes and green pepper chunks, or cook vegetables on separate skewers.

3   pounds boneless leg or shoulder of lamb
    Lemon juice
1   tablespoon salt
1   teaspoon each pepper and oregano
    Olive oil
    Tomatoes (optional)
    Green peppers (optional)

Cut lamb into 1½-inch cubes. Dip each cube in lemon juice. Combine salt with pepper and oregano; sprinkle over the meat cubes. Thread meat on skewers. Broil over charcoal until the meat is brown but still juicy, brushing with olive oil two or three times during the cooking. Makes 6 servings.

Pilaf-Stuffed Chicken Legs

Inexpensive chicken legs become special enough for company dinner when they are stuffed with a spicy rice pilaf. The stuffing is very easily pushed under the loose skin, which stretches so much that up to ⅔ cup of rice can be forced into each leg. This operation can be done ahead.

Begin baking the chicken about an hour before serving time.

1	medium-sized onion, chopped
1	cup long grain rice
2	tablespoons butter or margarine
1	teaspoon curry powder
¼	cup currants
2½	cups chicken broth
8	whole chicken legs (leg and thigh together)

Sauté onion and rice in butter or margarine until onion is just tender. Blend in curry powder and add currants. Stir in chicken broth, cover, and cook about 20 minutes, or until rice is tender. Cool.

To stuff chicken legs, carefully lift up skin of thigh; spoon about ⅔ cup rice under skin of each leg, keeping skin and membrane intact as much as possible. Use your fingers to push rice down leg. Wipe away excess rice and pull skin over opening. Arrange in greased baking pan. (Cover and refrigerate until baking if you wish.)

Bake the chicken legs, uncovered, in a 325° oven for about 50 minutes, or until chicken is just tender. Makes 8 servings.

Broiled Chicken Piquant

Broiled chicken is a calorie-saving dish, even though it is brushed with seasoned oil as it cooks to enhance flavor and crisp the skin.

3	whole chicken breasts, split lengthwise
	Salt and pepper
¼	cup olive oil
2	teaspoons prepared hot mustard
1	teaspoon basil
¼	teaspoon liquid hot-pepper seasoning

Sprinkle the chicken on all sides with salt and pepper. Shake together the oil, mustard, basil, and liquid hot-pepper seasoning; brush undersides of chicken with about half the oil mixture. Place skin-side down in a broiler pan without a rack. Broil for about 15 minutes, placing chicken about 8 inches from heat. Turn the chicken and brush with some of the remaining oil mixture.

Broil 10 to 15 minutes longer, brushing occasionally with drippings, or until tender and well browned. Makes 6 servings.

Coq au Vin

CHICKEN IN RED WINE WITH OLIVES

Pimiento-stuffed olives accent this smoothly seasoned chicken. Its flavor actually mellows with reheating. If you prefer, do not serve the chicken backs, wings, and necks to guests, but cook them as directed, as they enrich the flavor of the red-wine sauce.

3	large broiler-fryers (approximately 3 pounds each), cut up
½	cup butter or margarine
¼	cup brandy
1	bottle (about 3¼ cups) dry red wine
1	tablespoon salt
¼	teaspoon nutmeg
½	teaspoon dried rosemary, crumbled
1	bay leaf
1	tablespoon chicken stock base
3	cloves garlic, minced or mashed
1½	pounds fresh mushrooms (caps about 1 inch in diameter)
1½	tablespoons lemon juice
4	slices extra-thick-sliced bacon
2	cans (about 1 lb. each) small whole onions
2	teaspoons sugar
⅓	cup each cornstarch and water
1	jar (7 oz.) pimiento-stuffed olives

Using 2 large frying pans, brown chicken pieces in ¼ cup of the butter, turning to brown all sides. Warm brandy slightly, ignite 1 spoonful, and spoon flaming over the chicken; pour on remaining brandy and let flame over chicken. Pour in wine to loosen the browned drippings, then transfer chicken and liquid to a large baking dish or Dutch oven (about 8-quart size) with a cover. Add salt, nutmeg, rosemary, bay leaf, chicken stock base, and garlic. Cover and simmer gently for 1 hour, or until chicken is barely tender. Remove from heat.

Meanwhile, slice stems from mushrooms and leave caps whole; sauté stems and caps in the remaining ¼ cup butter along with lemon juice for a few minutes; transfer mushrooms and juices to the chicken.

Finely dice the bacon and, using the same pan, sauté until crisp; remove from pan and drain on paper towels. Pour off all but 2 tablespoons bacon drippings and add well-drained onions to the pan. Sprinkle with sugar, and heat, shaking pan until onions are lightly browned. Add browned onions to the chicken.

Blend cornstarch with water to make a paste. Drain the wine juices from the chicken into a saucepan and heat to boiling; stir in the cornstarch paste and cook until thickened, stirring constantly. Pour back over the chicken in the casserole. Add the drained olives and sprinkle with crisped bacon bits. (If made ahead, let cool and refrigerate at this point.)

Cover and reheat in a 350° oven for 30 minutes if prepared continuously or for 1 hour and 15 minutes if refrigerated. Makes 8 to 10 servings.

Danish Chicken and Meatballs au Gratin

This recipe epitomizes all that a good entrée for a special party should be. It is delicious, different (but not too different), and beautiful. Yet it is practical to make and serve at any time of year.

Almost all of the work is done ahead; at serving time you just assemble the meats and sauce in an ovenproof dish, and broil a few minutes until glazed and bubbly.

1	cup (½ lb.) butter or margarine
	Veal meatball mixture (directions follow)
2	large whole chicken breasts, boned and skinned
	Cooked sweetbreads (directions follow)
2	tablespoons each butter and flour
¼	teaspoon Dijon-style mustard
⅔	cup chicken broth (canned or freshly made)
½	cup whipping cream
⅓	cup dry white wine
1	cup shredded Danish Samsoe or Swiss Gruyère cheese
1	jar (4 oz.) sliced pimiento, drained
4	or 5 mushroom caps, lightly browned in butter (optional)
	Cherry tomatoes (optional)
	Parsley (optional)

In a small saucepan, heat the 1 cup bùtter until bubbly, but not browned. Scoop slightly rounded teaspoonfuls of the meatballs mixture and slide off spoon into hot butter. Cook several meatballs at once, turning as needed, just until browned, about 4 minutes. Drain meatballs on paper towels, then put into a 2-quart bowl; reserve the butter.

Slice chicken into ¼-inch-thick strips. Heat 4 teaspoons of the reserved butter in a frying pan and sauté chicken until white throughout; transfer to bowl with meatballs. Add butter to pan to make 2 tablespoons and sauté prepared sweetbreads until lightly browned; combine with meatballs.

For the sauce, heat the 2 tablespoons butter in a pan; add the flour and mustard and cook until bubbly. Gradually stir in broth, cream, and wine. Cook, stirring, until slightly thickened. Add cheese gradually, stirring, until melted.

Remove from the heat and stir in pimiento. (If you wish to serve later, cover and refrigerate sauce and meats separately.)

Just before serving, reheat cheese sauce. Add meat and cook slowly until heated through. Spoon into serving dish (one you can use in broiler), and broil about 5 inches from heat for 2 minutes, or until top is bubbly, but not brown. If you wish, garnish with mushroom caps, tomatoes, and parsley. Makes 6 servings.

VEAL MEATBALL MIXTURE. Combine in a bowl ¾ pound ground veal, ¼ cup flour, 1 egg, ⅛ teaspoon salt, dash of pepper, 2 teaspoons grated fresh onion, and ½ cup milk. Beat with a spoon until very smooth, cover, let stand at least 5 minutes.

SWEETBREADS. Wash 1 pound veal sweetbreads. Simmer in 1 quart water with 1 teaspoon salt and 1 tablespoon lemon juice for 15 minutes. Drain, rinse in cold water, drain again. Peel and cut away membranes; break into bite-sized pieces.

PLANNING THE PERFECT MENU

Many good cooks instinctively plan perfect menus, just as "primitive" artists paint masterpieces without training.

But the greatest works of art—or table—usually are the result of training, practice, and awareness of certain artistic principles. Many of the same principles a painter considers should also be considered by the menu-planner.

For example, color contrast and harmony. A meal in which all the colors are pale or dark, dull or bright, cannot be pleasing to the eye or stimulating to the appetite. Color is important.

Another element artists consider is texture. The perfect menu contains variety in this respect—some things are soft, smooth, spongy, or liquid; others are firm, chewy, flaky, crunchy, or crisp.

Artists also consider variety and harmony. The predominate flavors in the dishes served should rarely be the same, but they should be compatible. There should also be variety and contrast in other areas—consider both fresh or raw foods and cooked, aged, or dried foods; temperature variety (ranging from frozen through piping hot); both simple dishes and complex ones.

Other considerations in menu planning are practical, not artistic. You should estimate carefully the proper amount of food to prepare for your guests and the types of food pleasing to their tastes and diets. Select dishes which can mostly be made ahead. If last-minute cooking or baking is required, check that sufficient cooking units are available on top of the range and that oven space is sufficient.

The perfect menu is rarely an accident, but it is always a supreme pleasure to encounter.

Sesame-Soy Chicken

This chicken is first marinated in a teriyaki-type mixture of soy sauce, sugar, and ginger, broiled, and then coated in toasted sesame seed. Good either hot or cold, it could be a tasty change from fried chicken for a picnic or other outdoor meal.

2	pounds chicken legs and/or thighs
½	cup soy sauce
2	tablespoons sugar
1	teaspoon salt
	A 2-inch piece of fresh ginger, finely chopped
2	tablespoons sesame seed
	Melted butter or salad oil

Wash chicken and pat dry. Marinate for 1 to 2 hours in a mixture of the soy sauce, sugar, salt, and ginger. If you plan to barbecue the chicken at a picnic, put it into the marinade just before you leave home. Also toast sesame seed either in a frying pan or in the oven until lightly browned.

Remove chicken from marinade and grill over medium-hot coals in your broiler, brushing with some of the marinade and with melted butter or salad oil. Cook until nicely browned on both sides and the chicken is tender, about 30 to 40 minutes. Sprinkle with the toasted sesame seed when you remove it from the grill. Serve either hot or cold. Makes 4 to 6 servings.

Freezer Chicken Kiev

Chicken Kiev—butter-filled boneless chicken breasts fried in a crusty coating—makes a dramatic company main dish. But usually it has one drawback: last-minute preparation is required. However, there is a new way to prepare this entrée so you can do it almost entirely ahead, freeze it, then complete the cooking in the oven in just a few minutes with no attention required.

4	whole chicken breasts (3 to 3½ lbs.) boned and halved
1½	teaspoons crushed tarragon
	Salt and pepper
½	cup (¼ lb.) cold butter
	Flour
1	egg, beaten with 1 tablespoon milk
½	cup fine dry bread crumbs
	Fat for deep frying

Carefully remove skin from chicken so you do not tear flesh. Place chicken pieces, 1 at a time, between sheets of waxed paper. Pound gently with flat meat mallet until each piece is very thin and doubled in width. Sprinkle each piece evenly with tarragon, then lightly with salt and pepper. Cut butter into 8 sticks,

each about 2 inches long; place a stick at small end of each chicken piece.

Roll tightly, folding in sides to enclose butter and make a compact roll. Fasten with small metal skewers or wooden picks. Coat each roll lightly with flour, then egg mixture, then bread crumbs. Fry, 2 at a time, in deep hot fat (350°) for 5 minutes, until golden brown. Drain on paper towels; when cool, remove the skewers, wrap chicken rolls individually in foil, and freeze.

To serve, unwrap frozen rolls and let stand at room temperature for 1 hour. Bake on a rack in a shallow pan in a 450° oven for 20 to 25 minutes, until well browned. Makes 8 servings.

Barbecued Cornish Hens

Herb butter blends with a glistening apricot glaze to flavor these juicy Cornish hens. They should be cooked on a barbecue that can be covered; the surface of the grill should be large enough for heat to circulate around the pan holding the hens. They also may be oven-roasted.

4	frozen Rock Cornish game hens (12 oz. to 1 lb. each), thawed
	Salt and pepper
	Herb Butter (recipe follows)
2	tablespoons lemon juice
¼	cup warm, strained apricot jam
	Watercress sprigs and fresh apricot halves, for garnish

Wash Cornish hens; pat dry, inside and out, with paper towels. Sprinkle skin and cavities lightly with salt and pepper. Place about 1 tablespoon of the herb butter in large cavity of each; fasten cavities closed with wooden picks or small metal skewers. Tie legs together.

Melt remaining herb butter with lemon juice. Place hens, breasts up, on a double thickness of heavy foil; turn up a 1-inch rim on all 4 sides to form a shallow pan. Place on grill over glowing coals. Cover and barbecue, adjust drafts to keep fire burning slowly, and cook, basting occasionally with herb butter, for 45 minutes to 1 hour or until tender and golden brown.

If you wish to cook the birds in the oven, roast in 350° oven for about 1 hour.

When almost done, brush hens evenly with warm apricot jam; cover again and continue cooking until nicely glazed. Serve on wooden board or platter, garnished with watercress and fresh apricot halves. Makes 4 servings.

HERB BUTTER. Blend together ½ cup (¼ lb.) soft butter or margarine with 2 tablespoons chopped chives (fresh or freeze-dried) and ¼ teaspoon crushed rosemary.

Turkey Schnitzel

Treated in veal cutlet fashion, sliced boneless turkey breast is tender and flavorful. Marinate it first in an oil and lemon juice mixture.

    1   whole turkey breast (about 4 lbs.) split by
         meat dealer
    ¼   cup lemon juice
    ½   cup olive oil
    ¼   teaspoon each salt and pepper
    ½   cup flour
    1¼   cups grated Parmesan cheese
         Butter

Remove turkey from bone; skin, and cut meat crosswise into ½-inch slices. Pound slices slightly with a flat mallet to flatten to about ¼-inch thickness. Shake together lemon juice, olive oil, salt, and pepper. Pour over turkey slices in a shallow bowl; cover and refrigerate for about 1 hour. Drain turkey. Coat lightly with a mixture of flour and cheese. Quickly sauté turkey slices on each side in heated butter until lightly browned. Makes 6 to 8 servings.

Turkey Tetrazzini

This classic dish of slivered cooked turkey is so delicious that you may reverse the usual procedure, serving the first turkey meal to family and Leftovers Tetrazzini to the most special of guests.

    6   tablespoons butter or margarine
    5   tablespoons flour
    2½   cups chicken broth (canned or freshly made)
    1¼   cups half-and-half (light cream)
    ½   cup dry white wine
    ¾   cup shredded Parmesan cheese
    ¾   pound mushrooms, sliced
         Salted water
    8   ounces noodles (spaghetti or tagliarini)
    3   to 4 cups slivers of cooked turkey
         Salt

Melt 2 tablespoons of the butter, mix in flour and gradually blend in the chicken broth, cream, and wine. Cook, stirring, for about 3 minutes after mixture starts to simmer. Stir in ½ cup of the Parmesan cheese. Measure out 1 cup of the sauce and blend in remaining cheese.

Melt the remaining 4 tablespoons butter in a pan, add mushrooms, and cook quickly, stirring, until lightly browned. Bring a quantity of salted water to boiling, add noodles and cook until just tender to bite, but not soft; drain. Combine the large portion of sauce, mushrooms (save a few slices for garnish), hot noodles, and turkey; salt to taste. Turn into a large shallow casserole or individual casseroles.

Spoon the 1 cup of sauce evenly over the surface and top with reserved mushroom slices.

Bake in a 375° oven until bubbling; allow 15 minutes for large casserole and about 8 minutes for individual ones. Broil tops until lightly browned. Makes 6 to 8 servings.

Pheasant-in-a-Bag

When you roast pheasant inside a well-oiled paper bag, it stays juicy and acquires a beautiful reddish-brown color without basting. The classic Port wine sauce with orange peel makes a delectable accompaniment for any game bird.

    1   pheasant (2½ to 3 pounds)
         Salt and pepper to taste
    1   tablespoon pale dry Sherry
    1   small apple
    1   clove
         About 3 tablespoons salad oil

Season pheasant with salt and pepper to taste. Sprinkle the inside of the cavity with Sherry. Quarter apple, remove core, and stick clove in an apple piece. Place apple pieces inside the cavity and truss bird. Pour salad oil over a clean heavy paper bag until it is all coated. Place bird inside the bag; fold over the top and secure with 2 paper clips. Place in a roasting pan and roast in a 375° oven for 1½ to 2 hours, or until tender. Makes 3 to 4 servings.

CUMBERLAND SAUCE. Melt ½ cup currant jelly in the top of a double boiler over hot water. Stir in ⅓ cup *each* orange juice and Port wine. Mix together 2 tablespoons lemon juice, 1 teaspoon dry mustard, and ½ teaspoon powdered ginger and stir in. Remove peel from 1 orange and cover with cold water, bring to a boil, and drain. Scrape off any white membrane and cut peel into matchlike pieces, about ⅛ inch wide and ½ inch long. Add peel to sauce. Serve in a sauce bowl accompanying the pheasant.

Smoked Fish in Caper Cream Sauce

Serve the kippered salmon or cod on crisp toast points or in patty shells.

1	to 1½ pounds kippered salmon or kippered cod
2	tablespoons butter or margarine
2	tablespoons flour
1	cup half-and-half (light cream)
1	tablespoon chopped capers
4	prepared patty shells or 4 slices toast

Steam the kippered salmon or kippered cod in any kind of steamer, improvised if necessary. (Set fish on rack above boiling water, cover, and steam just until heated through. A 1-pound piece of fish takes 10 to 15 minutes.) Using two forks, flake into bite-sized pieces while hot, removing the bones.

Meanwhile, melt the butter or margarine in a pan; stir in the flour and cook until bubbly. Remove from heat while you slowly stir in the light cream. Add the chopped capers and cook, stirring, until the sauce is thickened. Stir in the hot fish. Serve in the patty shells or on crisp toast points. Makes 4 servings.

Individual Seafood Soufflés

Cold soufflés, unlike the hot kind, are not destined to fall sooner or later, because they are stabilized with gelatin. They are no more difficult to make than many gelatin salads, yet the cooked sauce and whipped cream within give a distinctive flavor and texture.

Make the soufflés ahead and garnish the sides with chopped olives right before serving.

2	envelopes unflavored gelatin
½	cup dry white wine
1	bottle (8 oz.) clam juice
1	can (10 oz.) frozen shrimp soup, thawed
4	eggs, separated
3	packages (6 oz. each) frozen king crab meat, thawed
⅓	pound cooked small shrimp
¾	cup whipping cream
	Chopped chives
	Suggested garnishes: cherry tomatoes, sliced cucumbers, hard-cooked egg halves, diagonally sliced celery sticks, carrot sticks

Sprinkle gelatin into a medium-sized pan, pour in wine and let stand until gelatin softens. Add clam juice and shrimp soup and heat until hot through. Beat egg yolks until light and gradually stir in part

of the hot soup mixture. Return to the pan, and cook a few minutes, stirring constantly. Cool, then chill until mixture starts to set.

Flake crab meat and reserve ½ cup for garnish. Mix in remaining crab meat and shrimp (save a few for garnish). Beat egg whites until stiff and fold in. Whip cream until stiff and fold in. Fold 8-inch strips of waxed paper into thirds lengthwise and place around six 3-inch individual soufflé dishes making 1½-inch collars; secure with paper clips. Spoon in soufflé mixture, letting it rise above the edge of the dishes 1 inch. Chill until firm.

To serve, run a knife between the edge of the waxed paper and soufflé mixture and remove paper collars. Press finely chopped chives onto the sides of the rims of each soufflé. Arrange reserved crab and shrimp on top. Place soufflés on salad-sized plates and surround each with several cherry tomatoes, cucumber slices, 1 or 2 hard-cooked egg halves, celery or carrot sticks. Makes 6 servings.

Freezer Seafood Newburg

This popular dish with Sherry-flavored cream sauce can be made from one or several kinds of shellfish. You freeze it in either large or individual casseroles, reheat without waiting for it to thaw.

Rice flour is used in part to thicken the sauce because it withstands freezing better than flour or cornstarch. It is sold in health food stores and Oriental markets.

2	cups (about ¾ lb.) coarsely chopped cooked lobster, crab, or shrimp
2	tablespoons butter or margarine, melted
1	tablespoon each flour and rice flour
¼	teaspoon each salt and paprika
	Dash each cayenne and nutmeg
2	cups half-and-half (light cream)
¼	cup dry Sherry (optional)
	Toasted English muffins or hot, cooked rice
	Chopped parsley

Arrange seafood evenly in four 4½-inch individual foil pans, one 8-inch foil cake pan, or a temperature-resistant 1-quart casserole. Drizzle evenly with melted butter. Mix flour, rice flour, salt, paprika, cayenne, and nutmeg in a small pan. Gradually stir in half-and-half to make a smooth mixture. Heat to simmering, stirring until thickened. Blend in Sherry. Pour sauce over seafood. Freeze quickly, then wrap well and store in the freezer.

To serve, bake uncovered in a 350° oven until sauce is hot and bubbly, about 30 minutes for individual casseroles or about 1 hour for a large one. Stir gently to blend sauce and seafood. Serve over toasted English muffins or cooked rice, sprinkled with chopped parsley. Makes 4 servings.

FISH—SIMPLY COOKED AND ELEGANTLY SAUCED

Fresh fish, simply cooked, then served with an appropriate sauce, is something you can offer with pride to your most discriminating guests.

COOKING THE FISH

Butter-sautéed, broiled, or barbecued fish is usually served hot, but poached fish is good either hot or cold. Cold, it's delicious in warm weather and easy on the hostess.

Butter-Sautéing. The French term is *à la meunière*. This method is most suitable for fillets of sole, flounder, or rockfish; for thin steaks of salmon or halibut; or for small, whole fish such as trout, perch, or smelt.

In a frying pan, heat butter, margarine, or part salad oil (¼ inch deep) until bubbly. Dip fish pieces in flour and sprinkle with salt and pepper. Sauté over medium-high heat until browned, turn, and brown other side—about 1 minute on each side for sole fillet, about 3 minutes on a side for trout.

Sauce Beurre à la Meunière. Sprinkle fish with chopped parsley. Add a little extra butter to the pan and brown lightly; add a few drops lemon juice and pour over fish immediately.

Poaching. This simple method is suitable for all types of fish. Much depends on having a good flavorful poaching liquid.

To prepare rich fish stock, ask your fish dealer for 1 to 2 pounds fish trimmings. Put fish trimmings into a large pan with 4 cups water (or 3 cups water and 1 cup white wine), 1 tablespoon lemon juice or vinegar, 2 teaspoons salt, 1 bay leaf, 1 medium-sized onion (sliced), 1 *each* carrot and celery stalk (sliced), a handful of parsley, and 3 whole black peppers. Bring to a boil, then reduce heat and simmer 1 hour. Let stand about 1 hour, then strain.

To poach fish, bring fish stock to a boil and pour over fish in a greased baking pan (or wrap fish pieces in cheesecloth and gently lower into the boiling stock). Cover pan and put into a 425° oven—or reduce heat and simmer on top of the range—until fish flakes when tested with a fork. Watch carefully. Small pieces take only a few minutes. Serve with a sauce.

Oven-Broiling. Any fish steak, fillet, or small, dressed, whole fish can be broiled. White, lean fish should be dusted lightly with seasoned flour, then sprinkled with melted butter; fat fish such as salmon, trout, albacore, or swordfish need only be basted well with butter.

Put either type of fish on a well-greased broiler rack or hinged broiler and place in a preheated broiler about 2 inches from source of heat for thin pieces, to about 6 inches for thick fish. Broil until browned and the fish flakes with a fork; fillets are broiled just on one side; steaks and whole fish should be basted, turned, and broiled until browned on other side; this takes 4 to 10 minutes, depending on thickness.

Barbecuing over Coals. Good choices are fairly thick fish steaks or fillets (salmon, albacore, sea bass, swordfish, sablefish) or small whole fish (trout or mackerel). Place on greased grill or hinged broiler over moderately hot coals. Grill, turning once and basting often, until fish is browned and flakes with a fork. Baste with melted butter; with equal parts butter and lemon juice; or with equal parts of butter, lemon juice, and Sherry or Vermouth.

FISH SAUCES

Hollandaise with Cucumber (for salmon, halibut, trout, albacore). Combine in the blender 3 egg yolks (at room temperature) and 1½ tablespoons lemon juice. Melt ¾ cup butter or margarine and heat until it bubbles—don't brown. Add 1 tablespoon hot water to the egg, turn blender on high speed, and immediately pour in hot butter in a steady stream (takes about 5 seconds). Add 1 teaspoon prepared mustard and ½ teaspoon salt and whirl until blended, about 30 seconds. Turn into a bowl and stir in 1 tablespoon *each* chopped parsley and chives, plus 1 peeled and seeded cucumber, chopped.

Hollandaise with Shrimp (for salmon, sole, halibut, sea bass, rockfish). Prepare preceding hollandaise sauce, except omit salt and cucumber. Stir in 1 can (about 5 oz.) shrimp (rinsed and drained).

Tomato Sauce (for halibut, rockfish, sea bass, swordfish, albacore). Sauté 1 medium-sized onion (chopped) in ¼ cup butter or margarine until soft. Add 1 crushed clove garlic, ½ teaspoon thyme, ¼ teaspoon crushed rosemary, and 1 can (1 lb.) stewed tomatoes (break up tomatoes with spoon). Simmer, uncovered, stirring occasionally, until reduced to about half—takes about 15 minutes. Add salt and pepper to taste.

Brown Butter Almond Sauce (for any fish, but best with salmon, halibut, trout). Heat 1 cup (½ lb.) butter until it turns a golden brown; cool to lukewarm. Into a bowl put 2 egg yolks, ½ teaspoon dry mustard, dash cayenne, and 1 tablespoon lemon juice; beat until blended. Slowly add the lukewarm butter (about 1 tablespoon at a time), beating constantly. As mixture thickens, you can beat in butter in a slow stream. Beat in 1 tablespoon *each* hot water and dry Sherry. Stir in ½ cup toasted, slivered almonds. If too stiff, beat in a little more hot water.

Kauai Fillet of Sole

Delicate sautéed sole entrées demand last-minute cooking to be at their best. When you prepare this Hawaiian-inspired sole and avocado dish, have ready the floured fillets, sliced avocado, and chopped macadamias. Have guests start eating salad; then cook the fillets in an electric frying pan right at the table, or on a serving cart.

    4   large sole fillets (1 to 1½ pounds)
         Salt and pepper
    2   tablespoons lime juice
         Flour
    3   or 4 tablespoons butter or margarine
    ¼   cup heavy cream
    1   large avocado, peeled, seeded, and sliced
             lengthwise
    ¼   cup coarsely chopped macadamia nuts
         Lime wedges

Sprinkle sole with salt and pepper and 1 tablespoon of the lime juice; let stand for 10 minutes. Dip fish in flour to coat all sides, shaking off the excess. At the table, heat about half the butter in an electric frying pan set at 350°; add fillets and brown about 3 minutes on one side. Turn fillets, add remaining butter, and cook until nicely browned. Remove fish to a warm serving platter and sprinkle with remaining lime juice. To the pan add the cream and bring to a rapid boil, scraping browned particles free; spoon over fish. Top with avocado slices and macadamia nuts; serve at once. Pass lime wedges. Makes 4 servings.

Clams Bordelaise

If you first start cooking the rice and then begin the clams, both should be ready to serve about the same time. Those who like plain steamed clams will find this dish equally pleasing in its simplicity.

    4   tablespoons butter
    4   tablespoons finely chopped parsley
    1   or 2 cloves garlic, minced or mashed
    2   cups regular strength chicken broth
    1   cup dry white wine (or ¼ cup lemon juice with
             ¾ cup chicken broth)
    3   dozen small hardshell clams, washed well
    1   to 2 cups hot, steamed rice

Heat the butter in a large, heavy pan. Add the parsley and garlic and sauté 1 or 2 minutes. Pour in the chicken broth and wine and bring to a boil. Add the clams, cover, and steam until clams open, about 5 to 10 minutes.

To serve, spoon some of the hot rice into each large soup bowl or soup plate. Arrange opened clams in each bowl, then pour over the broth and serve immediately. Makes 4 servings.

Brazilian Baked Trout

Victorious fishermen, who want to savor the freshness of the fish, demand it be cooked simply. This Brazilian treatment is subtle, using many of the traditional seasonings which bring out the natural flavor of the fish.

    4   to 6 medium-sized trout (about ½ pound each)
         Juice of 1 lemon
    1   teaspoon salt
    1   clove garlic, minced or mashed
    1   cup white wine
    2   tablespoons each chopped parsley, green
             onion rings, and dry bread crumbs
    4   tablespoons melted butter

Wash and dry trout with paper towels; rub outside with lemon juice and sprinkle with salt. Arrange the minced garlic in the bottom of a buttered, shallow baking dish large enough to hold trout in a single layer. Place trout in dish; pour wine over top. Sprinkle the parsley, green onion, and dry bread crumbs over trout; then spoon on butter. Bake in a 400° oven for 20 minutes. Serve from baking dish. Makes 4 to 6 servings.

Chafing Dish Scallops

These scallops with fluffy rice, green beans, flaky dinner rolls, and dry white wine will serve as lunch, supper, or after-theater meal.

Have the ingredients ready, and cook the dish before the eyes of your guests.

    ¼   cup (⅛ lb.) butter or margarine
    ¾   cup sliced unblanched almonds
    1½   pounds scallops
    ½   cup half-and-half (light cream)
    3   tablespoons finely chopped parsley
    ½   teaspoon salt
    ⅛   teaspoon oregano
         Dash pepper
    2   tablespoons dry Sherry
    1   tablespoon cornstarch
    1½   teaspoons lemon juice
         Hot cooked rice

Melt butter in blazer (top) pan of chafing dish over direct heat; add almonds, and cook until lightly browned. Stir in scallops; cook, gently stirring occasionally, until scallops lose their translucent look. Blend in half-and-half, parsley, salt, oregano, and pepper.

Blend the Sherry smoothly with cornstarch; stir into scallops and cook, stirring occasionally, until thickened. Blend in lemon juice. Serve with rice. Makes 4 servings.

Mushroom and Sausage Pie

For brunch, serve this pie with plain or cheese omelets; for lunch serve a tart green salad with it; for supper or dinner, let it accompany a roast of lamb or veal. The pie can be served either hot or cold.

  ½   pound bulk pork sausage
  1½   pounds small whole mushrooms
  ½   cup minced parsley
  2   eggs
  1   cup half-and-half (light cream)
  ½   cup shredded Parmesan cheese
  ¼   to ½ teaspoon salt
       Unbaked 9 or 10-inch pastry shell

Crumble sausage in a wide frying pan and add mushrooms. Cook over high heat, stirring frequently, until mushrooms and meat are lightly browned and all liquid from mushrooms has evaporated, about 15 minutes. Remove about 3 tablespoons of the sausage drippings from pan and discard. Mix parsley with mushroom mixture, return to heat and cook for 2 or 3 minutes.

Beat eggs with half-and-half and cheese, blend in the mushroom mixture, and add salt to taste; pour into pastry shell. Arrange mushrooms so that any stems showing are turned down into the liquid, and push the mushrooms down so pie is evenly filled. Bake on lowest rack in a 400° oven for 20 to 25 minutes, or until crust is well browned. Let the pie stand about 10 minutes before cutting. Makes 6 to 8 servings.

Jack Cheese Oven Omelet

This omelet requires no separating of eggs and beating of whites, but bakes to puffy perfection nevertheless. It makes a light meal for any time of day from breakfast to way-past-midnight.

  8   slices bacon, coarsely chopped
  4   green onions, thinly sliced
  8   eggs
  1   cup milk
  ½   teaspoon seasoned salt
  2½   cups shredded jack cheese (about 10 oz.)

Fry bacon until browned. Drain, reserving 1 tablespoon drippings. Sauté onions in drippings until limp. Beat eggs with milk and seasoned salt. Stir in bacon, onions, and 2 cups of the cheese. Pour into a greased, shallow, 2-quart baking dish. Bake, uncovered, in a 350° oven for 35 to 40 minutes until mixture is set and top is lightly browned. When almost done, sprinkle with remaining ½ cup cheese, and return to oven until cheese melts. Serve immediately. Makes 6 servings.

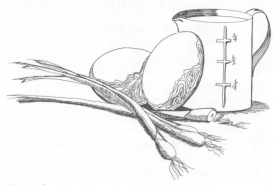

Chicken Livers and Mushrooms

Both chicken livers and fresh mushrooms are at their best sautéed. This quick dish is finished with a luscious sour cream and Sherry sauce made from the buttery pan juices.

  1¾   pounds chicken livers
  ¾   teaspoon salt
  ¾   pound mushrooms, sliced
  1½   cups sliced celery (cut on the diagonal,
         ⅜ inch wide)
  ½   cup chopped onion
       About ½ cup butter or margarine
       Flour
  ½   cup Sherry
  2   cups (1 pt.) sour cream
       Hot cooked rice
       Minced parsley

Have ready in the refrigerator, covered, chicken livers (cut in halves and sprinkled with about ¾ teaspoon salt), sliced mushrooms, sliced celery, and chopped onion.

To cook, place 2 wide frying pans over high heat and put ¼ cup butter or margarine in each. Add to one pan the mushrooms, celery, and onions. Dust chicken livers lightly with flour and place in the other pan (do not crowd). Cook the vegetables, stirring occasionally, until they are lightly browned; remove from heat and keep in a warm place. Brown chicken livers on all sides (you may need more butter) and add to vegetables as they are cooked. Pour Sherry into the pan in which the livers cooked, and bring to a boil, stirring to free browned particles. Reduce heat to low, and stir in sour cream; heat but do not boil.

Turn liver mixture into a serving bowl and pour the sour cream sauce over the top (or you can serve livers on the rice). Sprinkle liberally with parsley. Makes 6 servings.

Northern Italy Spaghetti

Make this long-simmered sauce ahead in a quantity to serve a very large group; reheat before serving.

1	pound round steak, cut into chunks
1½	pounds ground beef
1	teaspoon salad oil
4	cloves garlic, minced
2	medium-sized onions, chopped
1	green pepper, chopped
4	stalks celery, sliced
5	cans (6 oz. each) tomato paste
1	large can (1 lb. 12 oz.) whole tomatoes
1½	cups red wine
1	small bunch parsley, chopped
2	tablespoons dried basil
1	tablespoon each oregano and marjoram
1½	teaspoons thyme
½	teaspoon rosemary
3	whole black peppers
4	dried chile peppers, crushed
	About ¼ cup dried mushrooms
1	package (1 lb.) spaghetti, cooked

Brown the steak chunks and ground beef in the salad oil in a large frying pan; remove from pan. In the same pan, sauté the garlic and onions until golden, remove from pan. Then cook the pepper and celery until tender. Return these cooked ingredients to the pan and add tomato paste, whole tomatoes with liquid, wine, parsley, basil, oregano, marjoram, thyme, rosemary, black peppers, and chile peppers. Cover pan and simmer for 3 hours, stirring occasionally. Add mushrooms; simmer for 1 to 1½ hours more. Pour over cooked spaghetti. Makes 8 to 10 servings.

Basque Artichokes

Artichokes, filled with creamy scrambled eggs and surrounded by a tangy tomato sauce, are ideal for brunch or lunch.

6	medium-sized artichokes
	Boiling salted water
2	tablespoons lemon juice
3	tablespoons olive oil or salad oil
¼	cup chopped onion
1	clove garlic, minced or mashed
1	can (1 lb.) tomatoes
½	cup halved, pitted ripe olives
½	teaspoon each salt, thyme, and oregano
	Dash of pepper
	Grated Parmesan cheese

Slice off the top fourth of each artichoke. With scissors, cut thorns from tips of lower leaves. Peel stem and remove small leaves around base. With a small-bowled, long-handled spoon, carefully scoop out choke and a few of the center leaves to make a cup. Place artichokes in boiling salted water to cover; add the lemon juice and 1 tablespoon of the oil. Cover and cook until stems are just tender, about 30 minutes; drain. Cut off stems so artichokes will stand flat; chop and reserve stems for sauce. Stand artichokes in a baking dish.

Sauté onion and garlic in remaining oil until soft; stir in tomatoes, reserved chopped artichoke stems, olives, and seasonings. Bring to a boil, reduce heat, and simmer, uncovered, for about 20 minutes. Spoon sauce around artichokes in baking dish. Cover and bake in a 350° oven for 10 minutes or until artichokes are heated. Fill artichokes with Parsley Scrambled Eggs, serve with cheese. Makes 6 servings.

PARSLEY SCRAMBLED EGGS. Beat 6 eggs with 3 tablespoons half-and-half (light cream), ½ teaspoon salt, dash of pepper, and 2 teaspoons chopped parsley. Melt 2 tablespoons butter or margarine in a frying pan; scramble eggs in butter over low heat.

Chile Verde

This is a chile without beans, but definitely "con carne"—with *plenty* of meat. The *verde* (green) refers to the green chiles and bell pepper. Serve in bowls or spoon it over cooked rice.

1½	pounds each boneless beef chuck and boneless, lean pork shoulder, cut in 1-inch cubes
3	tablespoons olive oil or salad oil
1	green pepper, chopped
1	large clove garlic, minced
2	large cans (1 lb. 12 oz. each) tomatoes
1	large can (7 oz.) California green chiles, seeded and chopped
⅓	cup chopped parsley
½	teaspoon sugar
¼	teaspoon ground cloves
2	teaspoons ground cumin
1	cup dry red wine, or ¼ cup lemon juice and ¾ cup beef broth
	Salt

Brown about a quarter of the meat at a time on all sides in heated oil; remove with a slotted spoon and reserve. In pan drippings sauté green pepper and garlic until soft; add a little more oil, if needed.

In a large pan (at least 5 quarts) combine tomatoes and their liquid, green chiles, parsley, seasonings, and wine. Bring tomato mixture to a boil, then reduce heat to a simmer. Add browned meats, their juices, and sautéed vegetables. Cover and simmer for 2 hours, stirring occasionally. Remove cover; simmer for about 45 minutes more until sauce is reduced to thickness you wish and meat is very tender. Taste and add salt. Makes 6 to 8 servings.

Petite Marmite

BEEF AND VEGETABLE SOUP

Petite Marmite, "little pot," is really a full-meal soup, laden with succulent beef shanks, chicken livers, and assorted root vegetables. This version includes a special cheese that you lavishly sprinkle over each bowlful of soup.

3½	pounds beef shanks, cut 1 inch thick
3	quarts water
1	tablespoon salt
¼	teaspoon pepper
1	bay leaf
2	whole allspice
1	medium-sized onion, peeled
2	whole cloves
1	bunch carrots
2	turnips
3	stalks celery
3	leeks
½	pound chicken livers
1	tablespoon beef stock base or 3 beef bouillon cubes
2	tablespoons butter
¼	teaspoon paprika
3	tablespoons chopped parsley
1	cup shredded Parmesan cheese

Place beef shanks in a large soup kettle; add water, salt, pepper, bay leaf, allspice, and onion stuck with cloves. Bring to a boil, skim off frothy scum on top, cover and simmer 2 hours, or until meat is tender. Lift out meat and let cool.

Peel and slice carrots. Peel and dice turnips. Slice celery thinly on the diagonal. Slice leeks thinly. Add vegetables, chicken livers, and beef stock to broth and simmer 20 minutes. Remove bones and fat and dice the meat into bite-sized pieces. Add the meat to the soup.

Meanwhile make parsleyed cheese by creaming butter and mixing in paprika, parsley, and cheese. Reheat soup, ladle into bowls, and serve with the parsleyed cheese. Makes 8 servings.

Carmel Bouillabaisse

This Western version of the great seafood soup of southern France was created by the chef of a small French restaurant in Carmel, California. To make the bouillabaisse (boo-ya-bess) ahead, prepare and refrigerate the tomato base up to the point of adding the saffron. Before serving, reheat it, add saffron and fish, and simmer until fish are cooked. Serve the soup with steamed rice; each diner spoons some rice into his bowl as he makes room for it.

Sablefish is sometimes sold under the name of black cod or butterfish; salmon could be used in its place. Any rockfish may be used; other names for it are rock cod, red snapper, and Pacific ocean perch. If you're unable to obtain clams in shells, use canned ones, drained.

3	large cans (1 lb. 12 oz. each) tomatoes
½	cup water
1	teaspoon each salt and whole thyme
2	small bay leaves
¼	teaspoon white pepper
1½	pounds large shrimp or prawns
2	dozen small hardshell clams
½	pound scallops
4	frozen lobster tails, thawed
3	sablefish or salmon steaks (about 1½ lbs.), skinned and boned
1	pound rockfish fillets
⅛	teaspoon powdered saffron or ¼ teaspoon turmeric

In a large pan (about 5-quart size) combine tomatoes, water, salt, thyme, bay leaves, and pepper. Bring to a boil, reduce heat, and simmer, covered, for 20 minutes. Discard bay leaves; press tomato mixture through a fine strainer, reserving broth.

To prepare fish, shell and devein shrimp; rinse clams and scallops with cold water; cut lobster tails in half lengthwise; cut the sablefish and rockfish into about 1½-inch chunks.

Bring broth to a boil in a large deep pan (at least 6-quart size). Stir in saffron. Add shellfish and fish. Simmer, covered, for 10 to 15 minutes, or until shrimp and lobster turn pink and fish flakes easily. Remove from heat and loosen lobster meat from shells; return to fish mixture.

Serve the soup immediately, distributing some of all the fish into each bowl. Makes 8 servings.

FOLDED NAPKINS AND OTHER CUSTOM TOUCHES

At each guest's place in fine restaurants, often those with Continental influence, you may find a crisp starched napkin folded in an ornate shape. Such small details make dining more festive.

You can make a variety of fancy folded napkins at home with the instructions which follow. Other thoughtful touches might be: menu cards to let your guests know what courses to expect, especially appreciated when a sumptuous dessert is in the offing; individual salt dishes or salt and pepper shakers; a fresh flower tucked in napkin or laid beside silverware; several cigarettes, matches, and individual ash trays; fingerbowls with a floating lemon slice at the end of the meal; or steamy, damp finger towels in baskets Japanese-style.

Napkin-folding. With the following step-by-step directions and a little practice, you can be a master napkin-folder, turning out compliment-inspiring creations resembling fans, crowns, cones, and other interesting shapes.

White napkins are the most formal. You can also achieve lovely effects, especially for lunch or brunch, with colored, bordered, or print napkins.

Napkins today are usually smaller than in years gone by. If you have heirloom linens tucked away, this is the time to bring out grandmother's 22-inch-square napkins: the larger the napkin, the more dramatically it folds. Voluminous napkins aren't essential, however. You can do all these folds with more conventional 15 to 18-inch square napkins. But do use square napkins—most of the folds described cannot be accomplished otherwise.

To prepare napkins for folding, lightly starch them and press them flat (starch soft fabrics more stiffly). Store the napkins flat until you're ready to fold, then use a steam iron to press each fold (restaurant waiters don't do this, but ironing does help). You can prepare folded napkins hours or even days ahead.

For greatest success with the following instructions, read one step at a time and do that portion of the fold. Read the next bit and fold accordingly. If you continue this way throughout, you will produce a properly folded napkin with much more speed and less confusion.

Triangle. Fold in half away from you to make rectangle with fold toward you; fold left side over right one to make a square. Bring lower left corner to meet upper right corner, forming a triangle. Fold in half and stand napkin up with folded edge toward you.

Pyramid. Fold in half to make a rectangle with fold toward you. Bring upper right and left corners down to meet center of fold. Fold lower right and left corners up to meet at top edge. Turn over, end over end (by turning point facing you forward). Lift upper layer of bottom corner closest to you to meet top corner; lift center of this triangle into a peak, and cross bottom left corner over right corner.

Cone. Fold in half to make rectangle with fold at left; fold top edge down to bottom edge to make a square. To form a cone, start rolling tightly from lower left corner toward upper right one; keep point of cone at left and tightly rolled. Point will end at upper left corner, and wide open end at right. Turn up wide end forming cuff to hold napkin together.

Bishop's Hat. Fold in half to make a triangle with the point toward you. Bring upper left and right corners down to meet this point (the folded edges should come together). Fold the top corner down to within 1 inch of the point nearest you. Now turn this same corner back up to meet the last fold. Turn entire napkin over, and bring bottom corners together, tucking right corner inside left to hold in place. Stand.

Crown. Fold napkin in half to make a rectangle with fold toward you. Bring upper right corners down to meet center of fold, forming a triangle; bring lower left corner up to upper right corner to form a similar triangle. Turn over, with one of the new, long folded edges parallel to you. Fold edge closest to you to other edge, exposing a triangle at left, with point at bottom; turn over to expose two triangles whose points are at top. Tuck right end behind large left triangle; turn napkin over and repeat this to complete the crown. Stand upright.

Fan. Fold in half to make a rectangle with folded edge on left, open edges at right. Starting with short edge closest to you, crease in 1-inch accordion pleats. Pleat to within about 4 inches from top edge. Fold in half by turning the left half of rectangle underneath so that the pleats are outside and at the bottom. The folded edge will be at left. Turn down upper right corner, and tuck it behind pleat. Holding the tucked-in corner in one hand, place on table and spread the pleats into Japanese-fan shape. Use the portion with tucked-in corner as a stand at the back, which holds the open fan upright.

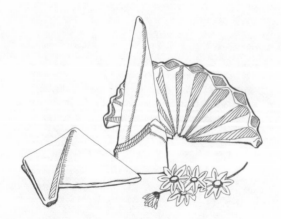

Salade Niçoise

SEAFOOD AND VEGETABLE SALAD PLATE

At restaurants along the French Riviera, Salad Niçoise is as much in demand as the mixed green salad in the western United States. The classic Niçoise (nee-swaz) is a vinaigrette of cooked potatoes and green beans, appetizingly arranged with tomato, olives, and anchovy fillets. But sweet red onions, pepper rings, radishes, cauliflower, asparagus, artichoke hearts, and a variety of seafoods can be added or substituted. The flavor of cooked ingredients improves if they are marinated a day or two. The salad can be assembled several hours before serving, and chilled.

¾	cup olive oil
¼	cup red wine vinegar
¼	teaspoon salt
	Freshly ground pepper
2	tablespoons each finely chopped chives and parsley
4	large boiling potatoes
	Boiling salted water
1½	pounds green beans
2	large tomatoes
2	or 3 hard-cooked eggs
10	to 12 anchovy fillets
½	cup pitted extra large ripe olives
1	tablespoon capers (optional)
	Butter lettuce
1	can (7 oz.) solid-pack white albacore tuna (optional)
	Watercress

For dressing, shake together oil, vinegar, salt, pepper, chives, and parsley; chill.

Cook unpeeled potatoes in boiling salted water 20 minutes, or until tender; cool immediately under cold water; peel and slice. Pour over just enough dressing to coat slices, mix lightly. Cover; chill at least 2 hours.

Cut off ends of beans and cut into 1½-inch lengths; cook in boiling salted water about 15 minutes or until crisp-tender; drain and cool immediately with cold water. Drain well again, then turn into a bowl and coat lightly with dressing. Cover and chill at least 2 hours.

Select a rimmed platter or large, shallow bowl and mound potato salad down the center. Arrange marinated green beans on each side. Peel tomatoes and cut in wedges. Quarter the hard-cooked eggs and alternate the egg quarters and tomato wedges beside the green beans. Criss-cross the anchovy fillets across the top of the potatoes.

Garnish with olives and sprinkle with capers. Cover with foil or clear plastic film and chill until serving time. When ready to serve, add a border of the inside leaves of butter lettuce and pour remaining dressing over them. Arrange tuna (in a round chunk, just as it comes from the can) on a side plate with watercress sprigs. Makes 4 servings.

Hawaiian Salad

Pineapple, papaya, and macadamia nuts are expected ingredients of this salad. The shrimp is a reminder of the sea and the pork of a luau, or perhaps the open-air Chinese shops in Honolulu where the roast meat hangs from hooks, a delicious sight.

FOR EACH SERVING:

	Spinach leaves
¼	pound cooked, shelled large shrimp or roast pork strips (or some of each)
3	slices fresh pineapple
3	slices papaya
1	tablespoon chopped macadamia nuts

For each serving, line a dinner plate with spinach leaves and finely chop several more leaves to make a nest in the center. Arrange on the plate shrimp or roast pork strips (or some of each), pineapple, and papaya. Chill. Garnish with nuts, add Curry Dressing. Makes 1 serving.

CURRY DRESSING. Blend ¼ cup each sour cream and mayonnaise. Mix in 1 tablespoon lemon juice, ⅛ teaspoon each dry mustard and garlic salt, and ¼ teaspoon curry powder. Chill at least 1 hour. Serves 2 or 3.

San Diego Salad

A salad named for San Diego would naturally be composed of foods much used in Mexican cookery—chicken, cheese, orange, avocado, olives, and tortilla.

FOR EACH SERVING:

	Romaine leaves
1	cooked split chicken breast
	Jack cheese (cut in strips)
	Several slices of salami
3	or 4 slices orange
3	slices avocado
	Several ripe pitted olives
	Wedges of crisp tortilla

For each serving, arrange outer romaine leaves on a dinner plate. Finely chop a few inner leaves and arrange on top. Bone chicken breast, cut in strips, and place on lettuce. Add jack cheese, several slices of salami, orange, avocado, olives, and triangular wedges of crisp tortilla. Cover and chill. At serving time add Cumin Dressing. Makes 1 serving.

CUMIN DRESSING. Blend ¼ cup each sour cream and mayonnaise, then add 1 tablespoon lemon juice, ⅛ teaspoon each dry mustard and garlic salt, ¼ teaspoon ground cumin, and 2 tablespoons canned green chile salsa or chile sauce. Chill. Serves 2 or 3.

Accompaniments and Side Dishes

THE PERFECT DINNER is perfect because of the attention given to every detail. Even the vegetables, bread, or other starchy accompaniments such as rice or pasta reflect planning and originality.

Vegetables prepared in a new way are always a delightful surprise. Some of the recipes in this chapter are classics. Others have been originated by creative cooks who believe vegetables deserve more attention than they are often given.

The rice and pasta recipes are largely foreign in origin. Fine ways of preparing these foods have been perfected over the centuries in countries where they are staples in the diet. Some you may want to serve as a separate course, the way they are presented in their native lands.

The bread recipes included here are those particularly adaptable for entertaining. Some are especially suitable for buffet or smörgåsbord use. A few are sweet, to go with ham, turkey, pork, and other meats which take well to such accompaniments.

Asparagus with Cashew Butter

Nuts always dress up a vegetable. Cashews here take the place of the almonds so often used with asparagus. The nuts are simmered with lemon juice and marjoram in melted butter, and the sauce is poured over the asparagus just before serving.

    1   pound fresh asparagus or 1 package (10 oz.)
            frozen asparagus spears
    ¼   cup butter
    2   teaspoons lemon juice
    ¼   teaspoon marjoram
    ¼   cup salted cashews, in lengthwise halves

Cook asparagus in salted water until tender, about 12 minutes, or if using the frozen asparagus, cook as directed on the package. Drain cooked spears and arrange on the serving dish. Meanwhile, melt the butter in a small pan; add lemon juice, marjoram, and cashews. Simmer over low heat for 2 minutes. Pour over the cooked asparagus and serve. Makes 2 or 3 servings.

Green Beans, Mediterranean Style

It's debatable whether these beans are better eaten hot or at room temperature. They are just as good the day after they're made as when freshly cooked. If you refrigerate them, either heat or let thoroughly warm to room temperature before serving.

    1   pound fresh green beans
    1   large onion, chopped
    4   tablespoons olive oil or salad oil
    ½   green pepper, seeded and chopped
    1   stalk celery, chopped
    ½   cup water

Remove ends and strings from green beans. Cut beans in 2-inch lengths. In a wide frying pan, cook onion in oil over high heat, stirring, until onion is soft but not brown. Add green pepper and celery; cook over moderate heat, covered, for 5 minutes; stir occasionally. Add beans and water to vegetables and continue to cook, covered, over moderate heat for 20 minutes, stirring occasionally. Makes 6 servings.

Green Beans with Water Chestnuts

Crunchy, sweet water chestnuts provide a pleasing contrast both in color and texture with the green beans in this recipe.

    ¼   cup (⅛ lb.) butter
    2   cans (5 oz. each) water chestnuts, drained
            and sliced (reserve liquid)
    1   teaspoon salt
    4   packages (9 oz. each) frozen cut green beans
        Butter or margarine

Melt butter in a saucepan; stir in the water chestnuts. Cook about 5 minutes. Blend in the salt and green beans. Using the liquid drained from the water chestnuts for liquid, cook the green beans until just tender, about 10 minutes.

Season to taste with butter, adding more salt if needed. Makes 8 to 10 servings.

Brussels Sprouts with Pecan Butter

Toasted pecans and strips of pimiento make this dish so festive you may want to serve it for one of the major holiday meals. Yet it is quick enough for enjoying any time.

    1½ pounds Brussels sprouts (about 2 pints)
        Salted water
    ⅓   cup chicken stock
    2   tablespoons chopped onion
    ½   teaspoon salt
    ½   cup sliced or chopped pecans
    ¼   cup butter or margarine
        Pimiento strips (optional)
        Parsley (optional)

Trim the Brussels sprouts and soak in salted water to cover for about 20 minutes. Drain and rinse with cold water. In a saucepan bring the chicken stock to a boil; add the sprouts, onion, and salt. Cook uncovered for 5 minutes; cover and continue cooking about 10 minutes, or until the vegetables are tender, but still slightly crisp. Drain, if necessary, and keep them hot.

Meanwhile in a small frying pan, sauté the pecans in butter for 2 or 3 minutes, until golden brown. Pour the butter mixture over the Brussels sprouts and mix lightly.

Turn the brussels sprouts into a serving dish and garnish with pimiento strips and sprigs of parsley. Makes 6 servings.

Limas and Peas Baked with Herbs

Basil is the herb used with these green vegetables. Delicate green onion also brings out their flavors.

    1   package (10 oz.) frozen baby lima beans
    1   package (10 oz.) frozen peas
    ¾   teaspoon each basil and salt
    2   green onions, thinly sliced (including part
            of tops)
    2   tablespoons butter or margarine
    2   tablespoons water

Thaw lima beans and peas for several hours at room temperature or in refrigerator overnight. Place in a greased 1½-quart casserole with basil, salt, and green onions; stir to blend. Dot with butter or margarine and sprinkle with water. Cover and bake in a 325° oven for about 45 minutes or until vegetables are just tender; stir occasionally. Makes 4 to 6 servings.

Beets with Mustard Butter

Beets are such a robust peasant-type vegetable that it is surprising they aren't more often sauced with something hearty. This recipe uses healthy quantities of mustard and vinegar.

    ¼   cup soft butter
    1   tablespoon prepared mustard
    1   tablespoon tarragon vinegar
    3   cups diced cooked beets

Beat together the butter, mustard, and vinegar. Heat beets, put in a hot vegetable dish, and add the mustard butter in small pieces. Mix lightly at table. Makes 6 servings.

Brandied Carrots

Turn pot roasts and stews into something special by ringing them with these brandy-flamed carrots. A fine roast of beef would also benefit from such an elegant garnish.

    10 or 12 slender carrots
        Boiling salted water
    3   tablespoons butter
    ¼   cup warm brandy

Scrape carrots. Cook in a small amount of boiling salted water in a wide, shallow pan until tender (about 10 minutes); drain off liquid. In the same pan or a chafing dish, melt butter; add brandy and set aflame. Sauté carrots until lightly browned, shaking back and forth to turn. Makes 4 servings.

Peas Cooked in Lettuce

Use a heavy frying pan or electric frying pan to cook peas this French way. You'll need a few large lettuce leaves. You can easily double this recipe; use two packages of peas, the same lining of lettuce leaves, and about the same cooking time. The lettuce leaves are discarded before serving.

Outside leaves from iceberg lettuce

- 1 package (10 oz.) small frozen peas, partially thawed
- ½ teaspoon salt
- ⅛ teaspoon pepper
- ¼ teaspoon whole fresh thyme leaves or pinch of dried thyme
- 1 teaspoon scraped or grated onion, or ½ teaspoon instant minced onion
- 2 tablespoons butter or margarine

Wash the iceberg lettuce leaves, shake off any excess water, and use them to line the bottom of a heavy frying pan (one with a tight cover) or an electric frying pan.

Empty a package of frozen peas; break any large pieces that are frozen together, and spread the peas on the lettuce. Sprinkle peas with the salt, pepper, thyme, and onion; dot the top with butter. Cover the pan, turn the heat to medium, and boil just until the peas are tender, about 3 minutes. Turn peas into a serving dish, discard the lettuce, and serve immediately. Makes 3 servings.

Nut-Crusted Squash Squares

A crunchy peanut and rice-cereal coating is a simple but surprisingly good addition to baked squash. Serve this hearty, rich vegetable with ham, pork, or poultry. You can prepare the squash and combine the peanut-cereal mixture in advance, then finish the cooking shortly before serving.

- 2½ pound piece of Hubbard or banana squash Water
- ⅓ cup finely chopped peanuts
- ⅓ cup crushed oven-toasted rice cereal
- ¼ cup brown sugar, packed
- ½ cup butter or margarine, melted

Remove seeds from squash and place, cut side down, in a shallow baking pan. Add hot water to a depth of ⅓ inch. Bake in a 375° oven for 45 minutes, or until almost tender. Cool and peel. Cut into 6 squares. In a bowl, mix together peanuts, rice cereal, and brown sugar; set aside.

About ½ hour before serving, dip squares in melted butter to coat all sides, then dip in peanut mixture, coating all over. Arrange in a shallow baking pan, cover, and bake in a 400° oven for 15 minutes. Uncover and bake 5 minutes more or until lightly browned. Makes 6 servings.

FANCY SHAPES FOR DINNER ROLLS

Hot yeast rolls for a dinner party may be made in one or more decorative shapes. They are easy to do using packaged hot roll mix.

Prepare the dough and let it rise the first time according to package directions. Shape rolls as described in the following instructions. (Each 13¾-oz. box of mix will make 12 large rolls or 16 smaller ones.) Let rise a second time, as long as the package recommends.

Bake large rolls for 12 minutes in a 400° oven, smaller ones 10 minutes. Baked rolls may be frozen.

Butterhorns. Roll dough to an 8-inch circle, ¼ inch thick. Brush with butter. Cut circle into 6 pie-like wedges, roll each toward point. Place on greased pan, point down. For Crescents, bend to shape like horseshoes.

Bowknots. Roll each piece of dough into a smooth, even rope, ½ inch in diameter and 10 to 11 inches long. Gently tie each length once, as you would to start to make a knot.

Snails. Roll each piece of dough into a rope about ½ inch in diameter and 10 inches long. Starting at one end, wind strip of dough around and around; tuck outside end firmly underneath roll of dough.

Braids. Form long ropes, each ½ inch in diameter. Braid 3 of the ropes into 1 long braid, cut it into 3½-inch lengths. Pinch the dough together at each end; pull the braid slightly to lengthen it.

Figure Eights. Roll each piece of dough into a rope about ½ inch in diameter and 10 inches long. Pinch the ends of the rope together, forming a loop; twist dough once to form figure eight.

Fan Tans. Roll dough to an 8 by 15-inch rectangle, ¼ inch thick. Spread with butter; cut into 5 lengthwise strips, 1½ inches wide. Stack the strips evenly; cut into squares. Put in greased muffin pans with cut sides up.

Celery Parmigiano

Celery, accented with Parmesan cheese, is baked just until golden to retain its characteristic fresh crispness.

3	medium-sized hearts of celery
	Water
1	teaspoon salt
½	cup grated Parmesan cheese
¼	cup butter or margarine, melted
¼	cup heavy cream

Wash celery and cut off top branches and leaves. Cut each heart in half lengthwise. Add celery to boiling salted water to cover. Reduce heat to low and cook for 20 minutes or until almost tender. Drain and place in well-buttered, 9-inch square baking dish. Sprinkle with the cheese. Combine butter and cream, and pour it over the celery. Bake, uncovered, in a 325° oven for 20 minutes, or until tender and golden. Makes 4 to 6 servings.

Spinach Pie

Vegetable pie, a refreshing variation on the casserole, can also be prepared in advance. This spinach pie is good hot or cold, either as a light entrée or side dish for roast meats such as chicken or turkey. Consider spinach pie the next time you must take a dish somewhere, such as to a potluck dinner.

1	small package (3 oz.) cream cheese, softened
1	cup half-and-half (light cream)
½	cup soft bread cubes, lightly packed
¼	cup shredded Parmesan cheese
2	eggs, slightly beaten
1	cup cooked (about 1¼ lbs. fresh) spinach, very well drained and finely chopped
4	tablespoons butter or margarine
1	large onion, finely chopped
½	pound mushrooms, finely chopped
1	teaspoon tarragon
	About ¾ teaspoon salt
	Unbaked 9 or 10-inch pastry shell

Mash cream cheese with a fork and gradually blend in half-and-half. Add bread cubes, Parmesan cheese, and eggs to cream cheese mixture and beat with a rotary mixer or wire whip to break up bread pieces. Stir in the spinach.

Melt butter in a wide frying pan and cook onion and mushrooms until lightly browned, stirring frequently; add tarragon when vegetables are soft. Blend hot vegetables with spinach mixture. Salt to taste.

Pour vegetable filling into pastry shell. Bake on lowest rack in a 400° oven for 25 minutes or until crust is well browned. Let stand 10 minutes and cut to serve hot, or let cool and cut to serve. Makes 6 to 8 servings.

Spiced Baked Onions

Onion fanciers will enjoy these tiny baked onions lightly spiced and topped with toasted almonds.

24	small white boiling onions
	Boiling salted water
3	tablespoons butter or margarine
1	tablespoon brown sugar
1	teaspoon salt
¼	teaspoon nutmeg or mace
6	whole cloves
	Dash each cayenne and white pepper
¼	cup toasted, slivered, blanched almonds

Peel onions; cook in boiling salted water for 5 minutes. Drain. Melt butter or margarine in a shallow 1½-quart baking dish; stir in brown sugar, salt, nutmeg or mace, cloves, cayenne, and white pepper. Add onions, stirring to coat with butter mixture. Cover and bake in a 325° oven for about 45 minutes or until onions are tender, stirring occasionally. Before serving, remove cloves, spoon some of the sauce over onions, and sprinkle with almonds. Makes 6 to 8 servings.

Squash à la Grecque

Two kinds of squash are colorful and tasty when cooked together, then seasoned the classic Greek way with olive oil and lemon juice.

6	each crookneck and zucchini squash
½	cup boiling salted water
4	tablespoons olive oil
2	tablespoons lemon juice
½	teaspoon crushed dried oregano
	Dash each salt and pepper

Cut off the ends of squash and slice in half lengthwise. Place in a saucepan with boiling salted water and simmer for 8 minutes, or until tender. Drain. Blend together olive oil, lemon juice, oregano, salt, and pepper. Pour dressing over hot squash. Makes 6 to 8 servings.

Ratatouille

MIXED VEGETABLE CASSEROLE

Ratatouille (rah-tah-*too*-yeh) is a summer vegetable stew that originated in the Midi, along France's sunny southern coast. The appeal of making ratatouille ahead is that it really tastes better after standing awhile. Serve it cold as a main-dish salad for hot weather, hot or cold as a meat accompaniment.

	About ½ cup olive oil
2	large onions, sliced
2	large cloves garlic, minced or mashed
1	medium-sized eggplant, cut in ½-inch cubes
6	medium-sized zucchini, thickly sliced
2	green or red bell peppers, seeded and cut in chunks
	About 2 teaspoons salt
1	teaspoon basil
½	cup minced parsley
4	large tomatoes, cut in chunks
	Parsley
	Sliced tomatoes (optional)

Heat ¼ cup of the oil in a large frying pan over high heat. Add onions and garlic and cook, stirring, until onions are soft but not browned. Stir in the eggplant, zucchini, peppers, 2 teaspoons salt, basil, and minced parsley; add a little of the oil as needed to keep the vegetables from sticking. Cover pan and cook over moderate heat for about 30 minutes; stir occasionally, using a large spatula and turning the vegetables to help preserve their shape. If mixture becomes quite soupy, remove cover to allow moisture to escape.

Add the tomatoes to the vegetables in the pan and stir to blend. Also add more oil if vegetables are sticking. Cover and cook over moderate heat for 15 minutes; stir occasionally. Again, if mixture becomes soupy during this period, remove cover to allow moisture to evaporate. Ratatouille should have a little free liquid, but still be of a good spoon-and-serve consistency. Add more salt if required. Serve hot or cold. Garnish with parsley and tomato. Makes 8 to 10 servings.

Tomatoes Stuffed with Spinach

Spinach, bacon, and bread crumbs comprise this hearty and colorful stuffing. Be sure to select ripe but very firm tomatoes about 2½ inches in diameter. Top tomato with sour cream just before serving.

6	medium-sized tomatoes
6	slices bacon
1	pound fresh spinach (or a 10-oz. package frozen chopped spinach)
¾	cup soft bread crumbs (whirl fresh bread in blender)
¼	teaspoon pepper
	Salt
	Sour cream

Cut a thin slice off tops of tomatoes and use a grapefruit knife to cut and scoop out centers (use the tomato pulp in other cooking). Turn tomatoes upside-down to drain. Meanwhile cook bacon until crisp; drain, crumble, and set aside. Also cook the spinach in the water that clings to leaves when you wash it, drain well, and chop. (Or cook the frozen spinach as directed, then drain well.)

Combine spinach, bread crumbs, bacon, and pepper. Sprinkle inside the tomatoes lightly with salt. Stuff the tomatoes with the spinach mixture and arrange them in a greased baking pan.

Bake, uncovered, in a 350° oven for 20 minutes, or until tomatoes are just tender but still hold their shape. Top each with a dollop of sour cream when you serve. Makes 6 servings.

Skillet Zucchini

Zucchini retain much of their color and firmness when sautéed with olive oil in a frying pan. Their high water content keeps them from browning too soon or toughening.

6	medium-sized zucchini
1	clove garlic, minced or mashed
3	tablespoons olive oil
1	tablespoon finely chopped parsley
1	teaspoon whole oregano, crushed
¾	teaspoon salt
¼	teaspoon sugar
⅛	teaspoon seasoned pepper

Slice zucchini about ¼ inch thick (do not peel). In a large frying pan sauté garlic in the oil for about 3 minutes. Add zucchini and cook, uncovered, over medium heat, stirring occasionally, for 8 to 10 minutes. Stir in a mixture of the parsley, oregano, salt, sugar, and pepper; cook for 3 to 5 minutes longer or until just tender. Makes 4 to 6 servings.

Potato-Onion Pancakes

These pancakes are good accompaniments to hearty main dishes, particularly those of German origin.

- ⅔ cup unsifted regular all-purpose flour
- ½ teaspoon salt
- 3 eggs, slightly beaten
- 1 cup milk
- 1 tablespoon each chopped parsley and freeze-dried chopped chives
- 1 cup shredded raw potato
- ¼ cup finely chopped onion

Combine flour, salt, eggs, milk, parsley, and chives; mix to blend. Let stand at least 30 minutes. Blend in potato and onion. Divide batter evenly into 4 floured, well-buttered, 9-inch foil pie pans. Bake in a 425° oven about 25 minutes or until browned. Fold in half and serve hot. Makes 4 servings.

Skillet Potatoes Anna

Sliced potatoes, baked with butter until crusty on top, are tasty with steaks and barbecued meats.

- ½ cup melted butter
- 6 to 8 large baking potatoes, peeled and sliced
  Salt
  Pepper

Brush a 10-inch heavy frying pan (one that can be put into the oven) or shallow baking dish with part of the melted butter and overlap the potato slices in the pan, sprinkling each layer with salt and pepper to taste. Pour over the remaining melted butter. Bake uncovered in a 450° oven for 45 minutes, or until the top is crusty and the potatoes are tender. Makes 10 servings.

Fluffy Potato Casserole

You can use leftover seasoned mashed potatoes or prepare instant mashed potatoes for this dish.

- 2 cups hot or cold mashed potatoes
- 1 large package (8 oz.) cream cheese, at room temperature
- 1 small onion, finely chopped
- 2 eggs
- 2 tablespoons all-purpose flour
  Salt and pepper to taste
- 1 can (3½ oz.) French-fried onions

Put the potatoes into the large bowl of your electric mixer. Add the cream cheese, chopped onion, eggs, and flour. Beat at medium speed until the ingredients are blended, then beat at high speed until light and fluffy. Taste, and add salt and pepper, if needed.

Spoon into a greased 9-inch-square baking dish. Distribute the canned onions evenly over the top. Bake, uncovered, in a 300° oven for about 35 minutes. (If you prepare this dish ahead, add the onions just before putting it in the oven.) Makes 6 to 8 servings.

Potato Parmesan Soufflé

Instant mashed potatoes speed the making of this impressive soufflé. If you need to hold the soufflé a few minutes before serving, leave it in the oven with the heat turned off.

- 8 servings instant mashed potatoes, prepared as package directs
- 6 eggs, separated
- ¾ cup shredded Parmesan cheese
- ½ teaspoon each salt and cream of tartar

Prepare instant mashed potatoes according to package directions for 8 servings. While still hot, beat in egg yolks, one at a time, and mix in cheese. (At this point, you can cover and let stand at room temperature a few hours.) About 1 hour before serving time, beat egg whites until foamy, add salt and cream of tartar, and beat until soft peaks form. Fold beaten whites into potato mixture. Spoon into two buttered 2-quart soufflé dishes or a 4-quart soufflé dish (or use baking dishes with straight sides.) Bake in a 375° oven, allowing 45 minutes for small soufflés or 1 hour for a large soufflé. Makes 8 to 10 servings.

Pecan-Topped Sweet Potatoes

A casserole of fluffy, orange-scented sweet potatoes, completely topped by pecan halves, can be a show-stopper. Put pecans in rows if your dish is square, or in concentric circles if round.

- 2½ to 3 pounds sweet potatoes or yams, cooked and peeled
- 2 eggs
- ¾ cup brown sugar
- ½ cup butter, melted
- 1 teaspoon each salt and cinnamon
  Orange juice (up to 1 cup)
- 1 cup pecan halves

Mash sweet potatoes (you should have about 6 cups). Beat in eggs, ¼ cup of the brown sugar, ¼ cup of the melted butter, salt, and cinnamon. (If potatoes seem dry, beat in orange juice until moist and fluffy.) Put in a 1½ or 2-quart casserole. (Refrigerate if you wish.) Before baking, arrange pecan halves on top; sprinkle with the remaining ½ cup brown sugar and drizzle with remaining ¼ cup melted butter. Bake, uncovered, in 375° oven for 20 minutes, or until heated through. Makes 8 to 10 servings.

Risotto

ITALIAN RICE

Unlike most other rice classics, Italian *risotto* has a creamy, flowing consistency. In Italy, it is served as the second or pasta course after the antipasto and before the meat or fish. But in American meals, risotto may come before, with, or after the entrée. For the best risotto, buy the best cheese and shred it yourself.

2   tablespoons each *butter or margarine and olive oil*
1   *small or medium-sized onion, chopped*
1   *small clove garlic, minced or mashed*
1   *cup long grain rice*
    About 3½ cups hot chicken or beef broth
    Salt to taste
½   *cup freshly shredded or grated Parmesan, Asiago, or domestic Romano cheese (or ¼ cup imported Romano)*
    About 1 tablespoon butter

Heat the 2 tablespoons butter and olive oil together in a Dutch oven, heavy 2-quart saucepan, frying pan with a tight-fitting lid, or flameproof casserole. Add the chopped onion and sauté over medium heat until golden. Add garlic and rice and stir until rice is milky in appearance, about 3 minutes.

Next add 1 cup of the broth, reduce heat, cover, and simmer until most of the liquid has been absorbed, about 10 minutes. Add the remaining hot broth in 2 or 3 additions, removing cover each time and stirring lightly with a fork; cook until the rice is tender and most of the liquid has been absorbed, about 20 to 25 minutes longer. (Exact amount of liquid needed and cooking time varies with rice and cooking pan you use.) Taste, and add salt if needed.

Remove from heat and add half the cheese and remaining 1 tablespoon butter; mix lightly with 2 forks. Turn into a serving dish or serve from the casserole, after topping with remaining cheese. You may also pass extra cheese. Makes 4 to 6 servings.

Wheat Pilaf with Peas and Lemon

Bulgur (cracked wheat) has been used for pilaf and salads in the Middle East for centuries. American-grown wheat, nearly identical to that used for bulgur, is available at most markets in the rice section, usually packaged in boxes. To simplify preparation, sauté the wheat and onion an hour or two ahead.

3   *tablespoons butter, margarine, chicken or bacon drippings*
2   *cups quick-cooking cracked wheat (bulgur)*
½   *cup sliced green onion*
    About 1 teaspoon salt
3   *cups chicken stock or other liquid*
1   *teaspoon grated lemon peel*
1   *to 2 cups frozen peas (thawed)*

Melt the butter in a large, heavy frying pan. Sauté wheat and onion in the butter about 5 minutes. Add salt (amount depends on saltiness of liquid used), liquid, and lemon peel; reduce heat, cover tightly, and simmer until the water is absorbed, about 15 to 20 minutes. Stir in peas 5 minutes before cooking is finished. (The wheat will still be quite crunchy; you may prefer to add as much as 1 additional cup liquid and cook it 5 to 10 minutes longer.) Makes 6 to 8 servings.

Note: Instead of cooking the pilaf on top of your range, you can transfer it to a greased casserole and bake it in a 400° oven. If the liquid in the recipe is hot when you add it, the pilaf will take about as long to bake as it does to cook on top of the range.

Green Noodles with Sour Cream

Green noodles, made with spinach, are cooked and put together quickly with the simple sour cream sauce. They make a colorful accompaniment for chicken or broiled fish steaks.

6   *ounces noodle-shaped spinach macaroni*
¼   *teaspoon onion powder*
½   *teaspoon salt*
2   *tablespoons milk*
3   *tablespoons freeze-dried chopped chives*
1   *cup sour cream*

Cook noodles in boiling, salted water until tender, about 8 minutes. Drain. Add seasonings, milk, and chives to sour cream and heat just until warmed through. Fold sour cream mixture into noodles, and serve immediately. Makes 4 to 6 servings.

Parsley Spaghetti

Butter, onion, cheese, and a liberal amount of fresh parsley make a colorful, quick sauce for spaghetti. This is a good dish for unexpected guests.

1   package (8 oz.) spaghetti
    Salted water
¼   cup butter
1   tablespoon olive oil
1   small onion, minced
⅔   cup chopped fresh parsley
½   teaspoon nutmeg
¼   teaspoon each salt and pepper
2   tablespoons grated Parmesan cheese

Cook spaghetti in boiling salted water as directed on the package; drain. Place on a platter and put in a 175° oven while you make the sauce.

Melt butter, add olive oil, and sauté the onion until it becomes translucent. Add parsley, nutmeg, salt, and pepper. Pour over spaghetti immediately. Sprinkle with cheese and leave in the oven for 5 minutes before serving. Makes 4 to 6 servings.

Egg-Foam Dumplings

Chicken stew makes a good companion for *nockerln*; you see the dumplings served this way in Austria and Switzerland. Remove the meat from the pot and keep it warm, then pour dumplings over the broth.

4   eggs, separated
⅛   teaspoon cream of tartar
½   teaspoon salt
4   tablespoons flour
    Chicken broth, canned or freshly made, or
      from a stew

Beat yolks until light and thick. Whip whites with cream of tartar until whites hold short distinct peaks; fold in salt, flour, and yolks. Have broth just below boiling point in wide pan (10 to 12-inch diameter); pour in foam. Cover, cook 3 to 4 minutes or until foam is set on top. Do not allow stock to boil actively.

Cut through foam with slotted spoon; lift sections from liquid, draining. Serve with prepared chicken dish or gravy. Spoon sauce over dumplings. Makes 4 to 6 servings.

FLAVORED BUTTERS FOR VEGETABLES AND FRENCH BREAD

Butter, flavored with herbs or other pungent seasonings, is an easy way to make vegetables outstanding. The butter may be prepared ahead and even molded into fancy shapes or balls (see page 18 for molding ideas). Just as you bring the serving dish to the table, put the butter on top. It will be pretty to see and good to smell.

Flavored butter has long been a favorite spread on slices of French bread before warming or toasting. At the end of each of the butter recipes to follow, it will be indicated when this particular kind is suitable for bread as well as vegetables. Each recipe also tells the kinds of vegetables most enhanced by this seasoning.

Flavored butters are not intended for long-time storage; for best flavor, plan to use them within a week or two.

For *each* of the following recipes, use ½ cup (¼ lb.) butter or margarine.

Fines Herbes Butter. Combine the butter and 1 tablespoon *each* minced parsley and chopped chives (fresh or freeze dried), ½ teaspoon *each* tarragon and chervil, ¼ teaspoon salt, and a dash of pepper; beat until fluffy.
Suggested use: Green vegetables; French bread.

Basil Butter. Combine in blender butter and ½ cup lightly packed, chopped fresh basil leaves (or 2 tablespoons dried basil), 2 tablespoons minced parsley, 1 tablespoon lemon juice, and ¼ cup grated Parmesan cheese; whirl until smooth (or crush basil and parsley with mortar and pestle, and beat together with other ingredients).

Suggested use: Spread on tomato slices before broiling; season baked potato, zucchini, eggplant, green beans, or green peas.

Red Onion Butter. Sauté 1 medium-sized red onion, finely chopped, in 2 tablespoons butter until soft, about 5 minutes; add 2 tablespoons dry red wine and cook until all liquid is evaporated. Cool thoroughly. Then combine onion mixture, the ½ cup butter, and ¼ teaspoon salt; whirl in the blender or beat until fluffy.
Suggested use: Fresh corn or almost any vegetable; French bread.

Maître d'Hôtel Butter. Combine the butter and 2 teaspoons *each* lemon juice and minced parsley, ¼ teaspoon *each* salt and thyme, and ⅛ teaspoon pepper. Beat until fluffy.
Suggested use: Many vegetables, especially carrots, onions, green peas.

Mustard Butter. Prepare Maître d'Hôtel Butter omitting thyme. Beat in 2 tablespoons Dijon-style mustard.
Suggested use: Asparagus, zucchini, or carrots.

Dill Butter. Press 2 hard-cooked egg yolks through a wire strainer; combine with butter and 4½ teaspoons dill weed, ½ teaspoon salt, and ⅛ teaspoon white or black pepper. Beat until fluffy.
Suggested use: New potatoes, carrots, green beans, or peas.

Upside-Down Lemon Muffins

Each of these lemon muffins is coated with a brown sugar and coconut mixture. Turn them out of the pans as soon as they're baked; serve upside down. They would make an interesting accompaniment to a fruit salad plate, roast turkey, or pork.

½   cup each *flaked coconut and firmly packed brown sugar*

2   tablespoons *flour*

3   tablespoons *melted butter*

⅛   teaspoon *nutmeg*

2   cups *regular all-purpose flour*

3   teaspoons *baking powder*

½   teaspoon *salt*

¼   teaspoon *nutmeg*

¼   cup *sugar*

1   *egg*

1   cup *milk*

3   tablespoons *melted butter or margarine, or salad oil*

1   tablespoon each *grated lemon peel and lemon juice*

Make coconut topping by blending coconut, brown sugar, the 2 tablespoons flour, 3 tablespoons melted butter, and ⅛ teaspoon nutmeg. Divide topping evenly into 12 well-greased 2½-inch muffin cups; press against bottoms and sides.

Sift and measure 2 cups flour; sift into a bowl with baking powder, salt, ¼ teaspoon nutmeg, and sugar. Beat egg lightly with milk, the 3 tablespoons butter or oil, lemon peel, and lemon juice. Stir milk mixture into dry ingredients just until combined. Fill prepared muffin pans about ¾ full.

Bake in a 400° oven for about 20 minutes or until well browned. Turn muffins from pans immediately; serve upside down. Makes 12 muffins.

Buttery Pan Rolls

Light and good tasting, these yeast batter rolls rise quickly. You can serve them right in the baking pan.

2   packages *active dry or compressed yeast*

½   cup *warm water (lukewarm for compressed yeast)*

4½   cups *regular all-purpose flour*

¼   cup *sugar*

1   teaspoon *salt*

6   tablespoons *butter or margarine, melted and cooled*

1   *egg*

1   cup *milk, scalded and cooled*

¼   cup *butter or margarine, melted and cooled*

Dissolve yeast in warm water and set aside until bub-bly. Sift flour, measure, and sift 2 cups of it with the sugar and salt.

Add 6 tablespoons butter or margarine, egg, yeast mixture, and cooled milk to the flour; beat at high speed with an electric mixer about 2 minutes. Then beat in the remaining flour by hand. Cover bowl and let batter rise in a warm place until doubled in bulk, about 45 minutes. Pour half of the ¼ cup melted butter or margarine into a 9 by 13-inch baking pan, tilting pan to coat the bottom. Beat down batter and drop by spoonfuls into the buttered pan making about 15 rolls.

Drizzle remaining melted butter or margarine over dough. Let rise in a warm place until almost doubled in bulk, about 30 minutes. Bake in a 425° oven for 12 to 17 minutes, or until the rolls are lightly browned. Serve hot. Makes about 15 rolls.

(You can also bake these rolls in muffin cups. Spoon about 1 teaspoon melted butter into each muffin cup. Fill cups half full; let batter rise until almost doubled. Bake as above.)

Pine Nut Sticks

These crunchy bread sticks go particularly well with a main-dish soup or salad served for a light lunch or supper.

1   package *yeast, active dry or compressed*

⅔   cup *warm water*

½   teaspoon *crushed anise seed*

2   tablespoons each *salad oil and olive oil*

¼   teaspoon *grated lemon peel*

1   teaspoon *salt*

1   tablespoon *sugar*

    About 2½ cups *unsifted all-purpose flour*

⅔   cup *pine nuts*

1   *egg, slightly beaten*

2   tablespoons *coarse salt*

Dissolve yeast in warm water; add crushed anise seed, salad oil, olive oil, lemon peel, salt, sugar, and 1 cup flour. Beat until smooth. Add pine nuts and another 1¼ cups flour, or enough to make a stiff dough.

Turn out on a floured board and knead until smooth and elastic (about 5 minutes), using additional flour as needed. Place dough in greased bowl, cover with damp cloth, and let rise in a warm place until doubled, about 1 hour.

Punch down, divide dough in half. Cut each half into 20 equal-sized pieces; roll each piece, using palms of hands, into a 7-inch length. Place parallel on greased baking sheets about ½ inch apart. Cover and let rise until almost doubled, about 30 minutes; brush with slightly beaten egg, and sprinkle lightly with coarse salt. Bake in a 325° oven for 30 minutes, until lightly browned. Makes 40 bread sticks.

Honey-Pecan Cornbread Sticks

A sweet honey-flavored syrup tops these pecan cornbread sticks when you turn them out of the pans right after baking.

⅓ cup plus 1 tablespoon firmly packed
    brown sugar
2 tablespoons each honey and butter or
    margarine
1 package (15 oz.) cornbread mix
¾ cup chopped pecans

In a small pan combine brown sugar, honey, and butter; stir occasionally over low heat until it boils and sugar is dissolved. Meanwhile prepare cornbread mix as directed on package. Sprinkle about 1 tablespoon chopped nuts into each of 12 average-sized cornstick forms; then spoon over about 2 teaspoons of the hot syrup. Divide cornbread batter into cornstick forms; bake 25 minutes or until lightly browned. Immediately invert onto serving platter; serve hot. Makes 12 corn sticks.

VARIATION: MUFFINS. Increase packed brown sugar to ¾ cup, honey and butter to 3 tablespoons *each*, and chopped pecans to 1 cup. Divide as above into 16 greased 2½-inch muffin cups. Makes 16 muffins.

Cheesy Spoonbread

Spoonbread will not suit some entertaining because it must be served right from the oven, like a soufflé. But in cases where the rest of the meal requires little last-minute attention, nothing is more delicious, especially when the main dish is cold meat or a salad.

1½ cups yellow cornmeal
1½ tablespoons sugar
¾ teaspoon salt
½ teaspoon chile powder
2½ cups milk
5 eggs
3 cups shredded cheese: Cheddar, Swiss,
    or jack

Stir cornmeal, sugar, salt, and chile powder into milk; set over simmering water and stir until smooth and thickened, about 15 minutes. Beat eggs with an electric mixer until thick and pale yellow. Stir in cornmeal mixture and 2½ cups of the cheese. Pour into buttered 1½-quart casserole with straight sides and sprinkle remaining ½ cup cheese over top. Bake in a 425° oven for 50 to 55 minutes or until top is lightly browned and wooden pick comes out clean. Serve at once for it will fall a little as it stands. Makes 8 to 10 servings.

Cheese Puff Ring

GOUGÈRE

The French serve *gougère* (goo-*zhair*) for lunch with a mixed green salad and red wine. However, you might serve this cheese-flavored, popover-type bread with barbecued meats for dinner. To double recipe, double ingredients in the dough; then bake two rings of seven puffs each. Extra baked rolls may be wrapped in foil and frozen; reheat in foil wrap.

1 cup milk
¼ cup butter or margarine
½ teaspoon salt
    Dash pepper
1 cup unsifted all-purpose flour
4 eggs
1 cup shredded Swiss cheese

Heat milk and butter in a 2-quart pan and add salt and pepper. Bring to a full boil and add the flour all at once, stirring over medium heat about 2 minutes or until mixture leaves sides of pan and forms a ball. Remove pan from heat and beat in (by hand) 4 eggs, one at a time, until mixture is smooth and well blended. Beat in ½ cup of the cheese.

Using an ice cream scoop or a large spoon, make 7 equal-sized mounds of dough in a circle on a greased baking sheet, using about three-quarters of the dough. (Each ball of dough should just touch the next one.) With the remaining dough, place a small mound of dough on top of each larger mound. Sprinkle the remaining ½ cup cheese over all. Bake on center shelf of a 375° oven about 55 minutes, or until puffs are lightly browned and crisp. Serve hot. Makes 7 puffs.

Whipped Cream Biscuits

In these fluffy biscuits, whipped cream is both the shortening and moistening ingredient. You can measure the dry ingredients ahead, then whip the cream and finish preparation just before serving.

1½ cups unsifted flour
¾ teaspoon salt
4 teaspoons baking powder
1 cup heavy cream, whipped

Measure flour, salt, and baking powder into a large bowl. Blend in the whipped cream with a fork until a stiff dough forms. Turn onto floured board and knead slightly. Roll dough out to about ½-inch thickness. Cut into rounds with a 2-inch cookie cutter. Place well apart on an ungreased baking sheet and bake in a 425° oven for 10 to 12 minutes, or until golden brown. Serve immediately. Makes 16 two-inch biscuits.

Distinguished Desserts

SOMETIMES YOU WANT to serve a simple, light dessert and other times an awe-inspiring creation. In this chapter you will find a great variety of sweets, most of which can be made partially or entirely in advance, often a day or more ahead. It is preferable to have as little work as possible to do on party day; and at dessert time especially, no hostess wants to spend many minutes in the kitchen.

Few standard recipes will be found here, and even the old familiars have new or intriguing treatments which make them exceptionally good.

Some helpful ideas for easy desserts using ice cream and fruits are included; lighter finishes to a meal are often most appreciated, especially when they satisfy the eye if not entirely the appetite.

Most of the dessert recipes may be prepared at any time of year, but some call for seasonal fruits. Often optional suggestions are included, making it possible to use what is available.

Pineapple Sherbet

This fruit-flavored sherbet is made with buttermilk, which contributes both to its tangy flavor and smooth texture.

To mellow the flavor, make the sherbet at least the day before you want to serve it.

    2   eggs, separated
    ¾   cup sugar
    1   can (9 oz.) crushed pineapple
    2   tablespoons lemon juice
    2   cups buttermilk
    1   teaspoon (part of a package) unflavored
           gelatin
    1   tablespoon water

Combine the egg yolks, ½ cup of the sugar, the pineapple (including the syrup), lemon juice, and buttermilk in the blender; whirl until blended (or beat together with rotary beater). Soften the gelatin in water; stir over hot water until dissolved; then blend into buttermilk mixture. Pour into a 2-quart container and freeze until firm around the outer edges of the container, about 1½ hours.

Beat the egg whites until soft, moist peaks form; gradually beat in the remaining ¼ cup sugar and continue beating until egg whites hold firm peaks. Break the partially frozen sherbet into chunks, pour it into a chilled bowl and beat until fluffy, then fold into egg white mixture.

Return to freezer container and freeze until it is firm. Makes about 1½ quarts.

VARIATION: RASPBERRY SHERBET. Follow recipe for pineapple sherbet but substitute 1 package (10 oz.) frozen raspberries, thawed, for the crushed pineapple. (If you do not have a blender, press the raspberries through a wire strainer, then beat together with the buttermilk, lemon juice, and ½ cup sugar.)

VARIATION: LIME-PINEAPPLE SHERBET. Follow receipe for pineapple sherbet but omit the 2 tablespoons lemon juice. Instead, add 1 can (6 oz.) frozen daiquiri mix or frozen lime concentrate, thawed, and 2 teaspoons grated lemon peel to the buttermilk mixture in the blender.

VARIATION: ORANGE SHERBET. Follow recipe for pineapple sherbet but substitute 1 can (6 oz.) frozen orange juice concentrate, thawed, for the crushed pineapple.

Chilled Zabaglione Cream

You can prepare this refreshing cream a day or two in advance and refrigerate it. This gives it an advantage over its namesake, frothy hot Italian Zabaglione, which must be made right before serving.

    6   tablespoons sugar
    1   teaspoon unflavored gelatin
    ½   cup Marsala or dry Sherry
    6   egg yolks
    1   tablespoon brandy or ¼ teaspoon brandy
         flavoring
    1   teaspoon vanilla
    ½   pint (1 cup) whipping cream
    3   egg whites
    ⅛   teaspoon each salt and cream of tartar
    ½   square (½ oz.) semisweet chocolate

Using the top of a double boiler, mix together 4 tablespoons of the sugar and the gelatin. Stir in wine. Beat egg yolks until light and lemon colored and stir in. Cook over hot water, stirring constantly, until thickened. Remove from heat and stir in brandy and vanilla. Cool.

Whip cream until stiff and fold in. Beat egg whites until foamy, add salt and cream of tartar, and beat until stiff. Beat in the remaining 2 tablespoons sugar. Fold meringue into the custard and spoon into tall, slender parfait glasses or dessert dishes. Chill for 1 hour or longer. Garnish with chocolate curls (use a vegetable peeler to make the curls). Makes 6 servings.

Meringue Shell Glacé

WITH FLAMING STRAWBERRY SAUCE

Expect this meringue shell to be soft and marshmallow-like; it simply melts when you bite into it. The suggested trio of ice creams makes a stunning combination with fresh strawberries and flaming berry sauce.

    5   egg whites
    ¼   teaspoon cream of tartar
    1¼   cups sugar
    1   teaspoon vanilla
    1   pint each vanilla, chocolate, and pistachio
         ice cream
    1   cup strawberries, washed and hulled

Place egg whites and cream of tartar in a mixing bowl and beat with an electric rotary mixer until foamy. Gradually add sugar, 1 tablespoon at a time, beating thoroughly after each addition; continue beating several minutes longer, until stiff and glossy. Beat in vanilla. Spoon into a well-buttered 10-inch pie pan, making a depression in the center.

Bake in a 300° oven for 1 hour, or until very lightly browned. Let cool. When made in advance, cool, then slip into a plastic bag and store in the freezer.

Scoop ice cream into small balls and refreeze. When ready to serve, let meringue shell thaw at room temperature and fill with alternating flavors of ice cream. Arrange 1 cup of whole strawberries between ice cream balls. Spoon Flaming Strawberry Sauce over ice cream. Makes 10 servings.

FLAMING STRAWBERRY SAUCE. Purée 1 package (10 oz.) frozen sliced strawberries, thawed (or 1¼ cups sliced strawberries mixed with ¼ cup sugar) in a blender until smooth. Then blend in 3 tablespoons undiluted orange juice concentrate and 1 tablespoon currant jelly. Turn into a small serving saucepan and add 1 cup fresh whole strawberries, washed and hulled. Heat sauce just until bubbly. Warm 1½ tablespoons *each* brandy and orange-flavored liqueur, ignite a spoonful, and spoon flaming over the strawberry sauce; then spoon over the remaining warm liqueurs.

Raspberry Torte

If make-ahead desserts appeal to you, this handsome freezer torte is ideal. You can make it days or even weeks ahead, and store it in the freezer (at 0° or colder).

    2   packages (10 oz. each) frozen raspberries
         (or 2½ cups fresh raspberries and
         sugar to taste)
    1¼   cups sugar
    ⅓   cup water
    1   teaspoon light corn syrup
    4   egg whites
    2   tablespoons kirsch (cherry brandy), optional
    2   cups (1 pt.) whipping cream
    1   package (3 oz.) ladyfingers (about 2 dozen
         split ladyfingers)
         Raspberries for garnish

Purée the berries in an electric blender. Press through a wire strainer to remove seeds, measure (you should have 2 cups purée), and add sugar to taste *only* if you have used fresh berries. Frozen berries need no extra sugar.

Combine the 1¼ cups sugar, water, and corn syrup in a small pan; bring to a boil and cook over high heat until the temperature reaches 238° (soft ball stage) on a candy thermometer. Beat egg whites with an electric mixer until soft peaks form, then gradually beat in hot syrup. Continue beating at high speed for 8 minutes, or until meringue mixture cools to room temperature. Fold in raspberry purée and kirsch. Whip cream until stiff; fold into meringue.

Line the buttered sides of a 9-inch cheesecake pan (a pan with removable bottom or spring-release sides) with split ladyfingers. Pour in the raspberry mixture. Cover and freeze until firm (8 hours or longer). To serve, remove pan sides, garnish the top with berries, and cut into wedges. Makes 12 servings.

Orange Shells Glacé

Scooped-out navel oranges, filled with citrus mousse and then frozen, make a handsome winter dessert.

- 9 medium-sized navel oranges
- 1 cup sugar
- 6 egg yolks
- 1 pint (2 cups) whipping cream
- 2 teaspoons vanilla
- 2 tablespoons lemon juice or orange-flavored liqueur
- 1 teaspoon each grated orange and lemon peel

Slice the tops off 8 of the oranges. Using a grapefruit knife, remove sections, holding the fruit over a bowl to catch the juice. Scoop out any remaining pulp with a spoon, then turn shells upside down to drain. Reserve the fruit for another purpose.

Measure ¾ cup juice; combine with sugar in a pan and cook until the temperature reaches 220° (jelly stage) on a candy thermometer. Place egg yolks in the top of a double boiler and slowly beat in the hot orange syrup with a portable mixer or rotary beater. Place over hot water and beat constantly until stiff peaks form, about 7 minutes. Remove from heat, place over cold water, and continue beating until cold.

Whip cream until stiff and fold in vanilla and lemon juice or orange-flavored liqueur, and the grated citrus peels. Fold into yolk mixture. Spoon mousse mixture into hollow orange shells, mounding the top. Cover; freeze until firm. To serve, thinly slice remaining orange and garnish. Makes 8 servings.

ELEGANT ICE CREAM FINALES

Ice cream is always a welcome end to a fine meal. The quality of ice creams you can buy is so great that dishes for the most discriminating can be created with little effort. Sometimes the secret of individuality is a sauce, other times molding with fresh or candied fruit. Following are ways to make ice cream desserts beautiful enough for the most special dinner party.

Cantaloupe Stuffed with Berries and Orange Ice. Select a large ripe cantaloupe for every 4 servings, and cut a 2-inch plug from the stem end. Discard seeds and stringy portions, and spoon out meat, leaving a good thick shell. Cut meat into pieces, and combine with about 2 cups sugared, sliced strawberries, raspberries, or blueberries. Flavor with a liqueur, if you wish. Chill melon shell and berries. Have ready 1 pint of soft orange sherbet; combine with berries, and fill melon shell. Replace plug and serve at once by slicing into quarters. Or you can put the filled melon in your freezer. Before slicing and serving, allow about 10 minutes at room temperature for it to soften.

Cherries Jubilee. Pack 1½ quarts slightly softened vanilla ice cream into a festive metal mold, or scoop ice cream into large balls; freeze. Drain the syrup from 2 cans (1 lb. *each*) dark Bing cherries into a saucepan. Add ⅓ cup currant jelly. Heat to boiling and stir in a blend of 2 tablespoons cornstarch and 2 tablespoons water; cook, stirring until thickened. Add cherries and heat through.

Dip mold into hottest tap water for about 10 seconds, then invert onto chilled serving plate. Return ice cream to freezer.

At serving time, reheat cherry sauce and take molded ice cream from freezer. Warm ⅓ cup kirsch (cherry brandy). At the table, ignite kirsch and spoon flaming over the hot cherry sauce; serve over the ice cream. Accompany with sweetened whipped cream and grated milk chocolate, if you wish. Serves 8.

Cassata. Line a 2-quart mold with 1½ quarts slightly softened vanilla ice cream; freeze until firm. Cover with a layer of 1 quart slightly softened chocolate ice cream; freeze until firm. Whip ½ cup heavy cream and fold in 1 teaspoon vanilla or 1 tablespoon maraschino liqueur. Beat 1 egg white until soft peaks form, and beat in 2 tablespoons powdered sugar; fold into cream. Then fold in 2 tablespoons *each* chopped candied red cherries, citron, and orange peel. Spoon into center of mold. Cover and freeze until firm.

To unmold the ice cream, dip the mold into hot water for about 10 seconds, then turn upside down over a cold serving plate. If it doesn't release immediately, repeat, dipping in water a shorter time. Refreeze 30 minutes before serving. Decorate with whipped cream, candied cherries, and citron. Serves 10 to 12.

Ice Cream in Chocolate Cups. Melt 1 package (6 oz.) semisweet chocolate pieces over hot but not boiling water. Using a pastry brush, spread chocolate evenly in 8 paper baking cups placed in 2½-inch muffin pans. Chill until hardened, about 2 hours. Carefully peel off paper; store chocolate cups in a cool place, or freeze until ready to use. Marinate ½ cup thinly sliced candied cherries in 2 tablespoons crème de cacao for 8 hours or more. Fill shells with 8 scoops vanilla ice cream to serve; top with cherries. Serves 8.

Ice Cream with Chocolate-Chestnut Sauce. Drain into a pan the syrup from 1 jar (7 oz.) chestnuts in vanilla-flavored syrup (marrons in syrup). Add 2 ounces semisweet baking chocolate and ¼ cup double-strength coffee. Stirring, heat until the chocolate is melted and sauce is smooth. Stir in 3 tablespoons rum, brandy, or Cognac. Slice the candied chestnuts and add to the sauce. Serve warm over coffee, toasted almond, vanilla, or chocolate ice cream.

Maple Parfait

CRYSTALLINE FROZEN CREAM

When you dip a spoon into this frozen dessert, you'll observe its distinctive crystalline structure. But when you taste, you'll discover a creamy texture. The dessert is much like ice cream, but its elongated crystals are the result of fast freezing without stirring.

- 4 eggs
- ⅛ teaspoon salt
- 1 cup sugar
- ½ cup water
- ½ teaspoon each maple flavoring and lemon juice
- 2 cups heavy cream, whipped

Using the large bowl of your electric mixer, beat the eggs with the salt until light and fluffy. In the top of a 2-quart double boiler, combine the sugar, water, maple flavoring, and lemon juice. Bring to a boil, over direct heat, and boil 3 minutes without stirring. Pour the hot syrup in a fine stream into the beaten eggs, beating constantly at a high speed. Pour this beaten mixture back into the top of the double boiler and cook over hot water, stirring constantly with a wooden spoon, until the mixture is slightly thickened (about 10 minutes).

Remove from the heat and set the pan in a bowl of cold water; continue beating until the mixture is cooled. Fold in the whipped cream and pour into a pan or mold; freeze quickly until firm. Makes about 1¾ quarts.

Cranberry Fruit Soup

Fruit soups are well known in the Scandinavian countries, Germany, Poland, and even in Oriental cuisine. The consistency varies from almost as thin as punch to as thick as cornstarch pudding; some are served hot, others cold. The thinner, tarter soups may be used just as a soup would be—before dinner. Those which are thicker and sweeter are best as dessert, as is this ruby-red, cold cranberry soup with whipped cream and almond garnish.

- 3 cups each cranberry juice and water
- ¾ cup sugar
- 6 tablespoons cornstarch
- 1 stick cinnamon
- 2 whole cloves
- Whipped cream
- Sliced almonds

Combine cranberry juice, water, sugar, cornstarch, cinnamon, and cloves in a pan. Bring to a boil; simmer, stirring, until juice is clear and slightly thickened. Chill. Serve in individual glasses; top with whipped cream and almonds. Makes 12 servings.

Orange Chiffon Soufflé

Orange juice concentrate and citrus peel flavor this low-calorie dessert. Cold soufflés, firmed with gelatin, do not fall as hot ones do. In fact, they must be made ahead.

- 2 envelopes unflavored gelatin
- 1 cup sugar
- Dash salt
- 2 cups cold water
- 6 eggs, separated
- 2 cans (6 oz. each) frozen orange juice concentrate, thawed
- ¼ cup lemon juice
- ½ teaspoon each grated orange and lemon peel
- ⅓ cup toasted slivered almonds
- Fresh strawberries (or other fresh fruit) for garnish

Mix gelatin, ¾ cup of the sugar, and salt in the top of a double boiler; stir in water and heat over direct heat until gelatin dissolves. Beat yolks of the 6 eggs until light and stir in the gelatin mixture. Return to the double boiler, place over a pan of hot water, and cook, stirring, until mixture coats the spoon. Remove from heat and stir in the orange juice concentrate, lemon juice, and grated citrus peels. Chill until it starts to congeal.

Beat the 6 egg whites until soft peaks form and gradually beat in the remaining ¼ cup sugar. Fold meringue into the chilled orange mixture. Fold a 20-inch length of waxed paper into thirds lengthwise and place around a 2-quart soufflé dish to form a collar; secure with paper clips. Spoon in the orange soufflé mixture, letting it come up above the rim of the mold. Chill until set.

When ready to serve, slip a knife between the waxed paper and soufflé and remove paper strip. Then press the almonds around the rim of the soufflé. Garnish with strawberries or other fresh fruit, and serve with chilled custard sauce. Makes 10 servings.

SOFT CUSTARD SAUCE. Scald 2 cups milk in the top of a double boiler. Beat 3 egg yolks until light and mix in ⅓ cup sugar and 1 tablespoon cornstarch blended together. Blend in the hot milk; return to the double boiler, and stirring constantly, cook until thickened. Stir in 1 teaspoon vanilla. Cool, then chill.

Sweet Country Cheese with Berries

This soft cheese is made from sour cream, eggs, sugar, and cream cheese, flavored with lemon peel. It is drained in cheesecloth, then molded into as simple or elaborate a shape as you wish.

    4   cups (2 pints) sour cream
    6   egg yolks
    1   package (8 oz.) cream cheese
    1   cup sugar
    3   or 4 strips lemon peel
         Strawberries
         Plain unsalted crackers

In the top of a double boiler heat sour cream, stirring, until scalding. Blend some of the hot cream with the egg yolks thoroughly beaten with cream cheese and sugar. Return all to double boiler. Add lemon peel. Cook over simmering water, stirring frequently, until thickened, about 15 minutes.

Remove from heat. Cover and let stand in the hot water for 15 minutes more; discard lemon peel. Line a large wire strainer or colander with 3 or 4 thicknesses of cheesecloth; arrange over another pan for draining. Pour in cheese mixture. Let stand about 2 hours at room temperature, then gently draw up loose edges of cheesecloth and fasten lightly over cheese. Continue draining while it chills overnight. Mold cheese or shape with a spatula. Serve with fresh strawberries and unsalted crackers. Makes 3 cups.

Hot Chocolate Soufflé

If you've shied away from a soufflé because you thought it difficult to make at the last minute, here's the way out: Make the cream sauce ahead of time—a soufflé is nothing but an egg-thickened cream sauce into which beaten egg whites have been folded. The sauce can stand as much as an hour, covered. About half an hour before serving, fold in beaten egg whites, and bake the soufflé.

    3   tablespoons butter or margarine
    ½   cup sugar
    2   tablespoons flour
    ¾   cup milk
    2   tablespoons cocoa
    3   eggs
    1   teaspoon vanilla
    ¼   teaspoon salt

Butter the bottom and halfway up the sides of a 1½-quart soufflé dish, or 5 individual baking dishes, with 1 tablespoon of the butter. Coat with 1 tablespoon of the sugar.

Melt remaining butter and blend in flour. Add milk gradually, and cook, stirring, until thick and smooth. Stir in cocoa and 2 tablespoons of the sugar. Separate eggs and beat yolks until thick. Add a little of the hot mixture to them, then combine the 2 mixtures. Cook a minute or so longer over low heat, stirring constantly, until mixture thickens again. Add vanilla. (This custard sauce may be made as much as an hour before the final preparation.)

Beat egg whites with salt until soft peaks form; then add remaining sugar gradually, and continue beating until stiff peaks form. Fold in chocolate sauce in 2 parts, and turn into the baking dish. Fit a "collar" (a 1½-inch-wide strip of paper 12 inches long) around the inside of the dish, if you wish, to make soufflé rise higher. Bake in a 400° oven 30 minutes for a large baking dish, 20 minutes for individual baking dishes, or until the soufflé feels set when touched lightly with your finger. Remove collar (if used) and serve at once. Makes 5 servings.

English Fruit Pudding

Mincemeat is usually associated with winter holidays, but its spicy fruit flavor is good in desserts at almost any time. This pudding resembles a pie (it's composed of a crust and filling), but is mound-shaped because you bake it in a bowl.

    2   cups unsifted flour
    2   teaspoons baking powder
    ¼   teaspoon salt
    ¾   cup butter
    7   to 8 tablespoons ice water
    1   can (1 lb. 12 oz.) prepared mincemeat
    3   cups chopped fresh apple
    1   cup chopped nuts
         Powdered sugar

Sift flour with baking powder and the salt into a bowl. With a fork, cut in butter until mixture resembles coarse crumbs. Stir in ice water, a tablespoon at a time, to make a dough that holds together in a ball. Turn out onto a lightly floured board and roll out to make a circle 14 inches in diameter.

Cut out exactly ¼ of the dough, just as you would cut a wedge of pie (a fourth of the pie); save to cover top of pudding. Fit the larger piece of dough into a buttered 1½-quart ovenproof bowl; moisten cut edges and press together to seal.

Prepare the filling by combining mincemeat, apples, and nuts; pour into the dough-lined bowl. Roll out the reserved fourth of the dough to fit top; place over filling, moisten edges, and seal. Prick top with a fork and bake in a 375° oven for 1 hour, or until golden. Cool 20 minutes, then invert onto serving dish; dust with powdered sugar. Makes 8 servings.

Souffléed Omelet

This hot dessert is not much like what its name implies. Although called an omelet, it is more like a tender egg pancake folded over thick meringue. Although called soufflé, it is surprisingly durable and will not fall.

    4   eggs, separated
    2   tablespoons sugar
    ½   teaspoon vanilla
         Dash salt
    2   tablespoons flour
    ¼   cup milk
         Butter
         Honey

Beat the egg whites until frothy; add the sugar, vanilla, and salt; beat until the mixture is satiny and will form stiff peaks; reserve.

Use a fork to blend the flour and egg yolks together; stir in milk until it is smooth.

Melt about ½ teaspoon butter in a 7½ to 8½-inch omelet pan and place over medium heat until butter browns slightly. Pour in ¼ of the yolk mixture (about 3 tablespoons) and spread it evenly by rotating pan.

Immediately spoon ¼ of the beaten whites on one side of the yolk layer; cook about 1 minute. Use a spatula to lift up the side *with* the beaten white filling and fold it over the free yolk side—it will only partially enclose the filling.

Cook about 1 minute longer so the whites will be heated through. Remove from the pan with a broad spatula.

Repeat process for each omelet, adding butter each time. Place cooked omelets in a 175° oven until all are cooked. Serve with honey. Makes 4 servings.

Pink Grapefruit Chiffon Pie

This pleasantly tart pie uses pink grapefruit juice; you can expect to squeeze ¾ to 1 cup of strained juice from a large grapefruit. The texture of the filling is refreshingly light.

    1   medium-sized pink grapefruit
    1   envelope unflavored gelatin
    1½   cups fresh pink grapefruit juice
    3   eggs, separated
    ¾   cup sugar
    ¼   teaspoon each salt and grated lemon peel
    ¼   cup lemon juice
    ½   teaspoon grated pink grapefruit peel
         Few drops red food coloring
    ¼   teaspoon cream of tartar
         Baked 9-inch pastry shell
         Sweetened whipped cream (optional)

Cut the peel and all the white membrane from grapefruit; lift out sections and drain well. Soften gelatin in 1 cup of the grapefruit juice. Beat egg yolks and combine in a pan with remaining ½ cup grapefruit juice, ½ cup of the sugar, salt, lemon peel, lemon juice, and grapefruit peel. Cook over low heat, stirring constantly, until mixture bubbles and lightly coats a metal spoon.

Remove from heat, add softened gelatin, and stir until gelatin is completely dissolved. Add a few drops food coloring to tint a medium pink. Chill gelatin mixture until it is thick enough to mound on a spoon. Beat the 3 egg whites with cream of tartar until frothy; add the remaining ¼ cup sugar and continue beating until stiff peaks form. Beat gelatin mixture until light and frothy. Fold in grapefruit sections, reserving several for garnish; then fold in the beaten egg whites. Spread in pastry shell; chill until firm, several hours or overnight.

To serve, garnish with reserved grapefruit sections and dollops of whipped cream, if you wish. Makes a 9-inch pie.

Mincemeat Cheese Pie

This pie has three layers—one of mincemeat, another resembling smooth cheesecake, and a topping of sour cream.

If you like to serve traditional dishes during the winter holidays, but still welcome them with a different twist, this recipe will provide just the right balance between the new and the old.

    4   packages (3 oz. each) cream cheese
    2   eggs
    ½   cup sugar
         Grated peel of 1 lemon
    1   tablespoon lemon juice
    2   cups mincemeat
         Baked 9-inch pastry shell
    1   cup sour cream
    2   tablespoons sugar
    ½   teaspoon vanilla
         Lemon slices

Beat together cream cheese, eggs, ½ cup sugar, lemon peel, and lemon juice with an electric mixer until very smooth. Spoon mincemeat into the baked pastry shell. Pour the cream cheese mixture evenly over the mincemeat.

Bake in a 375° oven for 20 minutes. Mix together sour cream, the 2 tablespoons sugar, and vanilla. When pie has baked the 20 minutes, remove from oven and spread sour cream mixture evenly over top. Return to oven for 10 minutes. Then chill pie before cutting and serving. Garnish with twisted lemon slices and lemon leaves (if available) just before serving. Makes 8 servings.

Pumpkin Ice Cream Pie

The filling for this pie is pumpkin mousse; you freeze it inside an ice cream "crust." Make it days ahead, if you wish, and remove it from the freezer a few minutes before serving.

1½	pints vanilla ice cream
1	cup canned pumpkin
¾	cup brown sugar, firmly packed
½	teaspoon each ground ginger and cinnamon
⅓	cup candied orange peel or mixed candied fruit, finely chopped (optional)
3	tablespoons rum (or ¼ cup orange juice)
¾	cup whipping cream
	Pecan halves for garnish

Put a 9-inch pie pan into the freezer when you remove the ice cream; allow ice cream to stand at room temperature a few minutes, until slightly softened. Then spread ice cream evenly over the bottom and sides of pie pan; set back in freezer if it gets too soft. Keep in freezer while you prepare the filling.

For the filling, combine pumpkin, sugar, ginger, and cinnamon in a saucepan. Stir over medium heat until mixture is just below the simmering point. Stir in candied fruit and rum (or orange juice); refrigerate until well chilled. Whip cream and fold into chilled pumpkin mixture. Pour into ice-cream-lined pie pan and freeze. Garnish with pecan halves just before serving. Makes a 9-inch pie.

Macadamia Cream Pie

A pie similar to this is one of the delights remembered by vacationers at a luxury hotel on Maui in Hawaii. This recipe combines the best qualities of a chiffon and a cream pie.

½	cup plus 1 tablespoon sugar
1	envelope unflavored gelatin
3	tablespoons cornstarch
¼	teaspoon salt
1	small package (3 oz.) cream cheese, softened
6	tablespoons sour cream
1¾	cups milk
2	eggs, separated
	About 1 cup (3¼ oz. jar) unsalted, chopped macadamias (see recipe for how to use salted nuts if unsalted ones are unavailable)
1	cup heavy cream
1	teaspoon vanilla
	Baked 9-inch pie shell

In the top of a double boiler, mix the sugar with gelatin, cornstarch, and salt (omit salt if salted nuts are used). Blend cream cheese with the sour cream until smooth; gradually stir in the milk. Slowly blend the liquid mixture into the dry ingredients in the double boiler. (Or combine sugar, gelatin, cornstarch, salt, cream cheese, and sour cream in a blender and whirl, gradually adding milk, until mixture is smooth. Put in double boiler.)

Cook over gently boiling water, stirring frequently, until very thick and smooth and about the consistency of a thick cream sauce, about 10 to 15 minutes. Blend some of the hot liquid with the egg yolks, then return to sauce. Cook, stirring, for about 2 minutes more. Remove pan from heat and take top of pan out of the hot water. Whip egg whites until they hold short, distinct stiff peaks, then fold the warm sauce into them. Chill until mixture is cool, but is not set.

Meanwhile, prepare macadamias. (Note: If unsalted, chopped nuts are unavailable, buy whole salted ones. Roll in a towel and rub to remove as much salt as possible; then chop.) To toast chopped nuts, spread them in an even, shallow layer in a pan. Bake in a 350° oven for about 5 minutes, shaking occasionally, until lightly toasted.

Whip heavy cream until stiff, and fold the cream, vanilla, and ½ cup of the macadamia nuts into the cooked mixture. Pour this filling into the baked pie shell; do not smooth top. Chill for 2 to 3 hours, then sprinkle remaining nuts over the surface of the pie and serve. Makes 6 to 8 servings.

Sweet Lemon-Yogurt Cake

In the eastern Mediterranean countries, yogurt is used for cooking and baking as often as we use milk or cream. Serve slices of this unfrosted Greek cake with ice cream or fruit. Cakes will keep several days if wrapped well.

1	cup (½ lb.) butter or margarine
2	cups sugar
6	eggs, separated
2	teaspoons grated lemon peel
½	teaspoon lemon extract
3	cups cake flour
1	teaspoon soda
¼	teaspoon salt
1	cup yogurt
2	tablespoons brandy (or substitute more yogurt)

Beat butter and 1½ cups of the sugar with an electric mixer until creamy. Add egg yolks, lemon peel, and lemon extract and beat until thick and pale yellow.

Sift the flour, measure, and sift again with the soda and salt. Into the creamed butter mixture alternately mix the flour and the yogurt (and brandy, if used). Beat the egg whites until soft peaks form; then gradually add the remaining ½ cup sugar, beating until glossy. Fold batter into beaten egg whites and pour into a greased 10-inch tube pan. Bake in a 350° oven for 45 minutes or until done. Cool 15 minutes in pan, then turn out on a rack. Makes 12 servings.

Four Seasons Cake

This delicious-looking cake makes use of fruit that is in season. It's made with a packaged angel food mix, fruit, and either lemon, lime, or orange-flavored filling.

In fall and winter, use grapes, pears, melons, papaya, pineapple, or oranges. In spring, try strawberries, papaya, melons, or grapes. Summer combinations are seeded, halved grapes with lemon filling; strawberry halves with lemon or orange filling; papaya or cantaloupe slices with lime filling; pitted, halved cherries with lemon or orange; peach slices with lemon; apricot slices with orange.

Any time of the year you can use well-drained canned or frozen fruits: pitted cherries, peaches, pears, apricots, or mandarin orange segments. (Dip fruit that darkens into an ascorbic acid mixture, following label directions; drain.)

1	package angel food cake mix
3	cups fresh, frozen, or canned fruit, well drained
1	envelope unflavored gelatin
¼	cup cold water
6	eggs, separated
	Dash salt
1	cup sugar
½	teaspoon grated lemon, lime, or orange peel
½	cup lemon, lime, or orange juice
1	cup heavy cream, whipped
	About ¾ cup fresh, frozen, or canned fruit, well drained, for garnish
	Fresh mint sprigs (optional)

Bake angel food cake according to package directions, using a 10-inch tube pan. Invert cake to cool; then remove from pan and wash pan. Prepare fruit and drain on paper towels.

Soften gelatin in water. In top of a double boiler, beat together slightly-beaten egg yolks, salt, ½ cup sugar, peel, and juice. Cook over hot water, stirring constantly, until mixture coats a spoon. Add gelatin and stir until dissolved. Set custard aside to cool, stirring occasionally. Beat egg whites until soft peaks form; gradually add remaining ½ cup sugar, beating until glossy. Fold slightly cooled custard mixture into egg whites.

Slice cake into 4 horizontal slices of equal width. Return bottom layer to tube pan, spoon ⅓ of the citrus filling over it, and arrange 1 cup of the fruit on filling. Repeat, using next two slices of cake and ⅓ of filling and 1 cup fruit for each layer. Add top cake slice, cover pan with foil, and refrigerate several hours or overnight.

Loosen cake from pan and invert on serving plate. Frost with whipped cream and garnish with fruit and mint, if used. Refrigerate.

To serve, slice the cake with a sharp knife. Makes 12 to 16 servings.

Finnish Old Times Cake

Bake the pastry layers ahead of time (wrap cooked layers individually in waxed paper, then overwrap in foil), but assemble cake just before serving. The layers are quite fragile so handle with care.

3	cups all-purpose flour
1½	cups (¾ lb.) butter
7	to 8 tablespoons cold water
	Sugar
2	packages (10 oz. each) sliced frozen strawberries, or 1½ cups fresh strawberries with ½ cup sugar
2	cups whipping cream
	Sugar
	Vanilla
	Whole strawberries

Sift the flour before measuring, put into a bowl. With pastry blender or 2 knives, cut in butter until particles are fine. Sprinkle in 7 to 8 tablespoons cold water, mixing with fork to form a dough. Gather together into a ball. On a floured board, roll dough into a log. Divide into 8 portions, graduated in size from about a 2-inch ball to a 4-inch ball. Roll out each into a circle about ¼ inch thick, using additional flour as needed to prevent sticking; keep unrolled portions chilled as you work (rounds should range from about 3 inches to 10 inches in diameter). Trim rounds into even circles with notched pastry cutter, if you wish. Place on lightly greased baking sheets. Prick all over with a floured fork. Brush surface of each very lightly with cool water and sprinkle with sugar (about 4 tablespoons altogether). Bake in a 375° oven for about 10 minutes or until golden; cool on wire racks.

Drain strawberries well. Whip cream with sugar and vanilla to taste. To assemble cake, place largest round on flat plate; top with a layer of sliced strawberries, then spread with part of the whipped cream. Repeat layering to make a pyramid-shaped cake, ending with whipped cream. Decorate, if you wish, with whole strawberries and fresh flowers. With a very sharp, thin-bladed knife, cut through top four layers to make wedge-shaped servings. Cut narrower wedges from bottom 4 layers. Makes 18 servings.

Sultana Raisin Cake

Expect this sultana cake to be compact, with a texture similar to that of pound cake. If tightly wrapped, it stays moist up to 4 days.

1½	cups golden raisins
	Water
1¼	cups butter or margarine
1½	cups sugar
5	eggs
1	tablespoon light rum
2	tablespoons lemon juice
2	teaspoons grated lemon peel
½	cup milk
3½	cups regular all-purpose flour
3	teaspoons baking powder
½	teaspoon each salt and soda
	Sifted powdered sugar

Cover raisins with water and let soak 30 minutes. In a large bowl, cream together butter and sugar. Add eggs, one at a time, beating well after each addition. Blend in rum, lemon juice, lemon peel, and milk. Sift flour; measure; sift again with baking powder, salt, and soda. Add gradually to creamed mixture.

Drain raisins; use paper towel to remove excess water. Mix into batter. Pour batter into well-greased and floured 10-inch tube cake pan or 10-cup mold. Bake in 325° oven for 1 hour and 20 minutes or until inserted pick comes out clean.

Cool in pan 10 minutes, then invert on rack; when completely cool, dust lightly with sifted powdered sugar. Makes 12 servings.

Persian Cardamom Cookies

These spice-scented treats from Iran have green pistachios pressed in their centers. The cookies are traditionally served with a refreshing cucumber punch (the recipe is on page 63).

¾	cup soft butter or margarine
½	teaspoon vanilla
1	cup powdered sugar
2	egg yolks
3½	cups cake flour
¾	teaspoon cardamom
	Pistachio nuts

Beat together butter or margarine, vanilla, and powdered sugar until fluffy. Beat in egg yolks, one at a time, beating until light colored. Sift and measure cake flour, sift with cardamom. Stir flour mixture into butter mixture until soft and well blended. Shape dough into ¾-inch balls. Press a small piece of pistachio in center of each. Bake on ungreased baking sheets in a 375° oven for 12 to 15 minutes, or until cookies are lightly browned. Makes about 4½ dozen.

Three Finnish Cookies

Here a basic dough is adapted in three different ways to make three kinds of different-tasting, beautifully shaped cookies.

They may be made ahead and frozen, ready for guests or holiday giving.

1	cup (½ lb.) soft butter or margarine
½	cup sugar
3	cups all-purpose flour

In a large mixing bowl, cream soft butter or margarine and sugar until light and fluffy. Sift flour before measuring, gradually beat flour into creamed mixture. Gather the crumbly mixture together; work between your hands until the warmth makes a smooth dough. Divide into three parts. Use one portion to make each of the following cookies:

RASPBERRY STRIP COOKIES. On a lightly floured board roll basic dough with palms of hands into logs about ½ inch in diameter and long enough to fit length of baking sheet. Place logs on lightly greased baking sheet.

With the side of your little finger, press a groove down the middle of each log, lengthwise. Bake in a 375° oven for 10 minutes. Remove from oven and fill groove with about 6 tablespoons seedless raspberry jam or other jam. Return to oven and bake 10 minutes more until dough is set and very light golden.

While still hot, brush with glaze made by mixing ½ cup powdered sugar and about 2 tablespoons water. Cut warm logs diagonally into cookies about 1 inch wide. Allow to cool on baking sheet on a wire cooling rack. Makes about 2 dozen cookies.

HORSESHOES. Thoroughly mix 1 egg yolk with ball of basic dough. Place dough into a cooky press fitted with a star tip. Force out long strips of dough onto board. Cut strips into 3-inch lengths; bend each to make a U-shape. Place on lightly greased baking sheet.

Bake cookies in a 375° oven for 12 minutes or until lightly browned. When cool, dip ends of horseshoes into 2 ounces semisweet chocolate, melted over hot water. Makes about 18 cookies.

CINNAMON HALF-MOONS. Thoroughly mix 1 egg yolk with basic dough. On a lightly floured board, roll out dough about ⅛ inch thick. With a circle cutter, cut into rounds 2 to 2½ inches in diameter. Cut each round in half. Place on lightly greased baking sheet, brush lightly with a beaten egg white. Sprinkle cookies with a mixture of ¼ cup sugar and ½ teaspoon cinnamon. Bake in a 375° oven for 12 minutes or until lightly browned at edges. Makes about 2 dozen cookies.

Orange Torte Cookies

This long, slender, log-shaped torte, filled with ground almonds and sugar, comes from Finland. You cut it into thin slices to make cookies.

  1½   cups all-purpose flour
  ¼   cup sugar
  ½   cup (¼ lb.) butter or margarine
  1   egg yolk
  2   teaspoons slightly beaten egg white
  1   cup ground almonds
  ¾   cup sugar
  ¼   cup sifted powdered sugar
      About 1 tablespoon orange juice
      Strips of candied orange peel
      Candied cherries

Sift flour, measure 1½ cups, and sift again with ¼ cup sugar into large mixing bowl. With pastry blender or two knives, cut butter or margarine into flour and sugar until particles are fine. Stir in slightly-beaten egg yolk. Gather the crumbly mixture together to form a ball; work between your palms for about 2 minutes or until the warmth of your hands makes a smooth dough. On a lightly floured board, roll dough out into a rectangle 5 by 10 inches.

Mix together slightly beaten egg white, almonds, and ¾ cup sugar. Turn mixture onto board; press together firmly to form a log about 8 inches long; place lengthwise down middle of dough rectangle. Bring up the two long sides of dough to encase the filling, overlapping edges slightly to seal; press to make a smooth seam. Pinch ends together to seal. Carefully lift filled roll onto a lightly greased baking sheet. Bake in a 400° oven for 15 minutes or until golden; cool. Drizzle top with icing made by mixing powdered sugar and orange juice. Decorate with orange peel and cherries. To serve, cut into thin slices. Makes 18 slices.

EASY FRESH FRUIT DESSERTS

Often fruit is the most welcome dessert after a meal of rich dishes.

A simple fruit dessert can be just as interesting as the rest of an elaborate meal. Following are some suggestions for attractive ways to present whole fruits, ways to use ice for chilling and eye-appeal, and delicious fruit combinations with wine, liqueurs, or sauces.

Strawberries, Oranges, and Champagne in Orange Shells. Slice off a little more than the top ⅓ section of 6 large navel oranges (each about 3 inches in diameter). Squeeze juice from tops and save; discard tops. With a grapefruit knife, cut fruit from each orange, carefully removing as large and whole a portion as possible. Cover shells and chill.

Cut fruit from membrane and place in a deep bowl. Squeeze juice from membrane into bowl and add juice reserved from the orange tops. Gently mix in 4 cups whole hulled strawberries, 1 cup chilled Champagne, and 3 to 4 tablespoons sugar (depending on sweetness of berries). Cover and chill at least 3 hours; stir carefully several times.

Mound fruits into orange shells. Set shells in individual serving dishes that are partially filled with crushed ice. Pour as much of the marinade as possible into each shell. Garnish with mint leaves and serve immediately. Makes 6 servings.

Fruit with Sour Cream Sauce. Gently stir into 1 cup sour cream, ½ cup powdered sugar, 1 teaspoon *each* grated lemon peel and lemon juice, and ¼ teaspoon vanilla. Cover and chill for several hours before serving. Spoon over fruit; sprinkle sauce lightly with nutmeg to serve.

Pineapple or Pears with Brown Sugar Rum Sauce. Beat yolks of 2 eggs until thick and light and gradually beat in ¼ cup brown sugar. Beat egg whites until soft peaks form and gradually beat in another ¼ cup brown sugar. Fold the yolk mixture into the meringue. Whip 1 cup heavy cream until stiff, stir in 2 tablespoons rum or ½ teaspoon rum flavoring, and fold into the egg mixture. Turn into a sauce bowl and dust the top with nutmeg. Chill. Serve over fresh sliced fruit.

Baked Apples or Bananas with Orange Cream Sauce. Place 1 cup heavy cream, 3 tablespoons frozen orange juice concentrate, and 3 tablespoons sugar in a bowl. Whip until stiff. Serve over hot baked fruit.

Fruit on Ice. For each serving, slightly mound finely crushed ice in a handsome dish or goblet. Top with sliced sugared fruit (such as peaches or figs) or small whole berries. Drizzle with a flavorful liquid such as a liqueur like Cointreau, rum, or fruit juice concentrate. Eat the fruit, then sip the chilled liquid through a straw.

Melon Mélange in Watermelon Shell. Combine 1 cup sugar and ½ cup water and bring to a boil; remove from heat and add ⅓ cup kirsch or Cointreau; chill. With melon ball cutter, make 10 cups assorted melon balls, or dice melon. (Suggested melons: cantaloupe, Casaba, honeydew, Persian melon, watermelon.) Just before serving, pile melon balls in watermelon shell or in a large serving bowl. Pour liqueur-flavored syrup over fruit. Garnish with sprigs of mint. Makes 10 to 12 servings.

Hot and Cold Drinks

MANY HOT AND COLD DRINKS, some unusual and some familiar, are described in this chapter.

Recipes are included for cool fruit and milk drinks suitable for young people or breakfast-brunch service. Sophisticated concoctions containing liqueurs and wines, many of which are rich and sweet enough to make a delightful substitute for dessert, are appropriate for adult meals or refreshment. Some exotic drinks from other countries will interest the adventuresome.

Both the cold and the hot, spicy wintertime punches will be convenient to serve at large parties.

You will also find a variety of recipes for coffee drinks from countries around the world. Some are rich enough to serve instead of a dessert, while others are meant to be black and strong finales to a heavy meal or a contrast to a very sweet pastry.

Lemon Frappé

Serve this sweet-tart and frosty beverage for dessert or for midday refreshment.

One ingredient is buttermilk; but since it loses its identity, you might keep it secret from anyone who is anti-buttermilk.

    1   cup whipping cream
    1   quart cultured buttermilk
    1½ teaspoons grated lemon peel
    4   tablespoons lemon juice
    ½   cup sugar
        Cinnamon or cinnamon sticks

Using a rotary beater, whip cream into soft peaks; set aside. Using the same beater, without washing it, whip buttermilk with lemon peel, lemon juice, and sugar until frothy. Fold whipped cream into buttermilk mixture, then pour into a chilled pitcher and serve in tall, chilled glasses.

Sprinkle a dash of cinnamon on top, or add a cinnamon stick stirrer to each glass.

If the beverage is made ahead and refrigerated, whip it with a rotary beater just before serving. Makes 6 to 8 servings.

Double Fruit Soda

Bottled berry syrup provides an excellent flavoring base for this fruit soda made with sherbet and ice cream. Use tall (12 to 14 oz.) glasses for each serving.

    ¾   cup bottled strawberry syrup
    ½   cup heavy cream, whipped
    1   quart club soda
    1   pint each orange sherbert, vanilla ice
          cream, and strawberry ice cream
    6   fresh strawberries for garnish
    1   orange, sliced with peel on for garnish

Place 2 tablespoons strawberry syrup in the bottom of 6 tall glasses. Spoon 2 tablespoons whipped cream into each and stir well with a spoon. Pour in about 2 tablespoons soda and stir until foamy. To each glass add 1 scoop *each* orange sherbet, vanilla ice cream, and strawberry ice cream. Pour soda into each glass, filling to the top, stir lightly, and add a dollop of whipped cream. Garnish each drink with a strawberry. Cut a slit just to the center of each orange slice and insert a slice over the side of each glass. Makes 6 servings.

Chocolate-Mint Fizz

The tang of soda water enhances the combination of chocolate syrup and peppermint ice cream.

- ½   cup chocolate syrup
- ¼   cup heavy cream, whipped
- 2   bottles (7 oz. each) club soda
- 1½   pints peppermint ice cream

Place 2 tablespoons chocolate syrup into the bottom of each of 4 glasses (about 10-oz. size). Spoon 2 tablespoons whipped cream into each and stir well with a spoon. Pour in about 2 tablespoons soda and stir until foamy. Add 2 scoops of ice cream to each glass. Pour soda into each glass, filling to the top, and stir lightly. Serve with straws. Makes 4 servings.

Fresh Fruit Yogurt Coolers

Now that fruit-flavored yogurt has become so popular, these drinks should be enjoyed by people who once regarded yogurt as a health food. Yogurt beverages are not a new idea; they have been popular in the Middle East for centuries.

- 1   cup sliced strawberries, crushed blackberries, crushed raspberries, or sliced peaches
- 1   cup cold yogurt
- 1   cup skim or whole milk
-     Sugar

Chill fruit. If you have no blender, force fruit through food mill or wire strainer; then blend with yogurt, milk, and sugar to taste. If you use a blender, whirl fruit, yogurt, milk, and sugar together until smooth. Then pour through strainer to remove seeds if raspberries or blackberries are used. Serve cold at once, or chill as much as 3 hours. Makes 3 cups.

Milk Punch

Usually such a punch is a cold-weather drink, but ice is added to this version to make it refreshing for hot weather—or any season.

- 1   cup brandy
- 2   cups cold milk
- 6   tablespoons powdered sugar
- ½   teaspoon vanilla
- 6   to 8 ice cubes, coarsely crushed
-    Nutmeg

Pour brandy into blender with milk, sugar, vanilla, and crushed ice cubes. Whirl the mixture until it is frothy and well blended. Pour into glasses or punch cups; sprinkle with nutmeg. Makes 4 to 6 servings.

Alexander Icicle

Soft ice cream blended with liqueurs is fun to sip through straws. Be sure you chill the glasses well so the ice cream won't melt.

- 1   pint vanilla ice cream, softened
- 2   tablespoons each crème de cacao and brandy

Put the ice cream and liqueurs into a chilled blender container. Blend just until smooth. Pour into chilled small glasses or sherbet glasses. Add short, fat straws. Makes 4 servings.

Kahlua Frost

Coffee liqueur and coffee ice cream give smooth flavoring to this summery beverage for grownups.

- 4   tablespoons Kahlua or other coffee-flavored liqueur
- ¼   cup heavy cream, whipped
- 2   bottles (7 oz. each) club soda
- 1   pint coffee ice cream
- 4   cinnamon sticks

Place 1 tablespoon Kahlua in the bottom of 4 large (8 oz. size) wine glasses or sherbet glasses. Add 1 tablespoon whipped cream to each glass and stir until blended. Pour about 2 tablespoons soda into each glass and stir until foamy. Add 1 large scoop of ice cream to each glass and pour in sufficient soda water to fill to the top. Add a dollop of whipped cream and insert a cinnamon stick into each glass to serve as a stirrer. Makes 4 servings.

Mexican Chocolate

Mexican hot chocolate is beaten until frothy, spiced with cinnamon, topped with whipped cream, and spiked with a cinnamon-stick stirrer.

- 6   cups milk
- ¾   teaspoon cinnamon
- 6   ounces coarsely chopped sweet cooking chocolate
- ½   cup heavy cream, whipped
- 2   tablespoons sugar
- 6   cinnamon sticks

Heat milk with the ¾ teaspoon cinnamon until steaming. Add chopped chocolate and stir until melted. Beat with a rotary mixer until mixture is frothy. Have ready heavy cream, whipped stiff with the sugar.

Pour hot chocolate into cups and top each with a spoonful of the cream. Drop a cinnamon stick in each cup if you wish. Makes 6 servings.

Ginger Wine Punch

Lemon slices and sprigs of mint float on the top of this light amber, sparkling punch, which is shown off at its best in a clear glass bowl.

A large block of ice keeps the punch chilled without diluting it too much; you might wish to freeze a few additional lemon slices in the ice for additional decoration.

    2   bottles (1 qt. each) ginger ale, chilled
    3   bottles (4/5 qt. each) Sauterne, chilled
    3   sprigs mint
    1   whole lemon, thinly sliced

In a large punch bowl, mix together the chilled ginger ale and chilled wine. Place mint sprigs and lemon slices on the top for garnish. Add a chunk of ice to keep punch chilled. Serve in punch cups. Makes 22 to 24 servings.

Sangria

This popular Spanish punch is made with red wine, orange and lemon juice, and sparkling water.

    1   whole orange
    1   whole lemon, thinly sliced
        Juice of 1 lemon
    2   bottles (4/5 qt. each) Burgundy or Pinot Noir
    ½   cup sugar
    1   bottle (1 qt.) sparkling water, chilled

Cut the outer rind from the orange in a spiral strip, removing as little of the white membrane as possible. Then squeeze orange juice. In a large bowl, mix together the orange spiral, orange juice, lemon slices, and lemon juice. Add the Burgundy and sugar. Stir until sugar is dissolved. Chill at least 4 hours. Remove lemon slices and orange peel. Pour into punch bowl; add sparkling water. Makes 12 servings.

COFFEES FROM AROUND THE WORLD

Because of the coffee houses which have become popular throughout the West and the frequency of foreign travel, most guests will be familiar with (and appreciative of) any foreign coffee you choose to serve.

Italian Caffé Espresso. You need an espresso machine, which forces water and steam under pressure through finely ground, dark, Italian-roast coffee, or you can prepare a reasonable facsimile using an Italian *macchinetta* (sometimes called Neopolitan or *caffettiera*) or a pressurized Domus espresso pot.

Follow the manufacturer's directions. Serve in demitasse cups with sugar (raw or refined)—never with cream!

For *Espresso Romano*, pour coffee into small, stemmed, heat-proof glasses and garnish with a twist of lemon peel. To make *Cappuccino*, combine coffee with an equal amount of milk heated on an espresso steam valve. Or quickly pour coffee into an equal amount of hot milk, and stir until foamy. Serve in slender Cappuccino cups and sprinkle with cinnamon.

French Café. In specialty food shops and some supermarkets, you can purchase a tin of French-roast coffee. Make in a drip pot, or by the individual cup with French coffee filters.

The French use two pots to make their *café au lait*. One is filled with a strong, hot French coffee, the other with an equal amount of hot, rich milk. Taking a pot in each hand, you pour from them simultaneously into a cup.

Viennese Coffee. Brew extra-strength coffee, pour into cups, and top with a drift of sweetened whipped cream. Dust the cream lightly with powdered nutmeg or cinnamon.

Caffé Borgia. The Italians probably named this drink after the aristocratic Borgia family of the 15th and 16th centuries. Pour equal parts hot chocolate (made with milk) and double-strength coffee into heated cups. Top with a heaping spoonful of lightly sweetened whipped cream; sprinkle with grated orange peel and shaved bittersweet chocolate.

Russian Coffee. In the top of a double boiler, melt ½ ounce semisweet chocolate over hot water. Add ¼ cup sugar, ⅛ teaspoon salt, and ¼ cup water. Place over direct heat and simmer for 5 minutes, stirring. Add ½ cup *each* milk and whipping cream (or 1 cup half-and-half) and heat, but do not boil. Add 2 cups hot, strong, freshly made coffee, and 1 teaspoon vanilla. Beat with a rotary beater until foamy and serve immediately. Serves 4.

Dutch Koffie. Place a cinnamon stick in each serving cup, fill with freshly brewed black coffee, stir in 1 tablespoon whipping cream, and float a pat of butter on top. Serve with sugar.

Irish Coffee. Into a warmed table wine glass, place 2 teaspoons of sugar; fill glass about ⅔ full of strong, hot coffee. Stir. Add 2 tablespoons of Irish whiskey, and top with softly whipped cream. Makes 1 serving.

Mexican Coffee. For this Mexican dessert coffee, spice 1½ cups strong black coffee with ½ teaspoon cinnamon; sweeten to taste and top each demitasse cup with a generous dollop of sweetened and spiced whipped cream. (Use ¼ teaspoon *each* nutmeg and cinnamon with ½ cup whipping cream.) Makes 4 demitasse servings.

Persian Cucumber Punch

Iced cucumber punch—from Iran, where cucumbers are regarded as fruits—is refreshingly tart on a warm afternoon. To garnish the punch bowl for a party, make an ice ring with unpeeled cucumber and lemon slices frozen in it.

        6   medium-sized cucumbers
        2   cups Punch Base (recipe follows)
        8   cups cold water
        ¼   cup lemon juice

Peel, quarter, remove seeds, and coarsely chop cucumbers. Whirl about ⅓ at a time in blender until puréed; strain out and discard pulp (you should have about 2½ cups juice). Just before serving, mix 2 cups Punch Base (recipe follows), 8 cups cold water, cucumber juice, and lemon juice. Pour over ice to serve. Makes 3 quarts punch.

PUNCH BASE. Combine 1 cup water, 3 cups sugar, ¾ cup cider vinegar, and ½ cup lemon juice; bring to a boil and cook until syrup reaches 230° on candy thermometer (spins a 2-inch thread). Remove from heat and add chopped mint; cool. Strain; store in a covered jar. Makes about 2 cups.

Spicy Citrus Punch

You can make this tea-based punch ahead; serve it cold or reheated.

        4   quarts water
        1   tablespoon whole cloves
        1   teaspoon whole allspice
        2   sticks whole cinnamon
        6   lemons
        6   oranges
        ⅓   cup tea leaves
        3   cups sugar
             Orange for garnish (optional)
        6   whole cloves (optional)

Put 2 quarts of water in a pan and add the 1 tablespoon cloves, allspice and cinnamon. Using a vegetable peeler, remove the thin outer zest from peel of the lemons and oranges; reserve the fruit. Add fruit peel to spices; cover, bring to simmering. Reduce heat and steep (below boiling point) for 30 minutes. Meanwhile bring remaining 2 quarts water to boiling, remove from heat, add tea, cover, and steep for 10 minutes. Strain both mixtures and combine; while still hot, stir in the sugar until dissolved. Add the juice of the lemons and oranges (strained). If made ahead, refrigerate until needed.

Reheat to serve hot; garnish with a small whole orange, stuck with about 6 whole cloves. Or serve the well-chilled punch over ice in a punch bowl; garnish with the orange slices. Makes about 40 servings.

Glögg

In American Scandinavian communities, glögg (pronounced "glug") is well known. It's the traditional hot Christmas drink of Sweden. Whole clove-studded baked oranges floating in the punch contribute flavor and also garnish the punchbowl.

        6   oranges
             About 6 dozen whole cloves
        1   cup warm rum
        1   gallon (4 quarts) hot apple cider
        3   sticks cinnamon

Stud each whole orange with 10 to 12 whole cloves. Place on a baking pan and bake in a 300° oven for 2 hours, or until juices start to run. Transfer to a heatproof 2-gallon serving bowl (or copper pan). Pour over warm rum, ignite, and flame. Then pour in hot apple cider and add cinnamon sticks. Keep hot over a warmer during serving time, ladling into small heatproof punch cups. If you wish, stir in additional rum. Makes about 32 servings.

Cider Wassail Bowl

This hot and spicy cider punch has roasted apples bobbing on top, the way they are served on the traditional English wassail of ale or wine.

        3   tablespoons light corn syrup
        3   tablespoons sugar
        ¼   teaspoon cinnamon
        8   lady apples (or 5 small red cooking apples)
        2   quarts apple cider
        1   lemon, thinly sliced
        1   stick cinnamon
        4   whole cloves

Heat corn syrup in a small pan; combine 3 tablespoons sugar with ¼ teaspoon cinnamon in a shallow dish. Roll each apple in hot syrup, then in the sugar; arrange on a baking pan, and bake in a 400° oven until partially cooked, about 15 minutes (apples should not lose their shape).

In a large pan, heat slowly over very low heat to just below boiling point the apple cider, sliced lemon, stick cinnamon, and cloves. Before serving, strain out the spices and add the roasted apples. Serve piping hot. The small lady apples may be served in the punch cups. Makes 12 servings.

Special Meals for Special Occasions

THE MENUS AND PARTY PLANS offered in this chapter are not great in number, but they are varied. Some are very simple and easy to arrange; a few are exotic enough to challenge the confident and experimental cook. Some are intended for elegant occasions, others for very informal get-together, perhaps out-of-doors. Some are definitely for adults; others are suitable for groups of all ages, or young people.

Different ways of entertaining are represented. Most involve full meals: those planned around one important main dish, those of several courses served at the table, those presented buffet-style, and those served out-of-doors. Others are ways to entertain without a complete meal—snacks, beverage parties, and informal occasions where the guests may pitch in to help make what they eat. These informal party ideas are particularly useful for the younger set, but most will also have appeal for adults.

Barbecued Ham Buffet

FOR EIGHT TO TEN PEOPLE

CHARCOAL-BARBECUED HONEYED HAM

HOT CARROT-ASPARAGUS PLATTER

GRAPEFRUIT-AVOCADO SALAD

HOT CRESCENT ROLLS

PINEAPPLE SHERBET

Recipe on page 50

This buffet has two noteworthy features: The ham is barbecued on a covered grill, and the vegetables are combined on a special platter that's both attractive and easy to serve. Most of the menu can be prepared in advance. You might serve cranberry juice cocktail to guests in the living room as the first course.

CHARCOAL-BARBECUED HONEYED HAM

Often it is helpful to prepare the meat outside for a meal served indoors; this frees the oven for baking and prevents the house from being filled with cooking odors. Remember to baste the meat occasionally during the final hour.

	Tenderized or fully cooked ham
3	tablespoons honey
1	tablespoon Worcestershire
1	tablespoon dry mustard
¾	teaspoon ground ginger
	Dash of black pepper

Place a drip-catching pan in the fire bed beneath grill where the ham will be placed. You can make one of heavy-duty foil folded double. It should be about 3 inches longer and 2 inches wider than the ham, with sides about 2½ inches high.

Start two charcoal piles (one on either side of the drip-pan) of 20 briquets each, 30 to 45 minutes before you plan to start the ham (the briquets should burn down to an even gray). After each hour of cooking time, add about 6 briquets on each side.

Start the ham on the grill 3 to 5 hours before serving time, depending on the size and type of ham you buy. Plan on 15 to 20 minutes per pound if you buy a "tenderized" ham (or cook to 160° on a meat thermometer); or 10 to 15 minutes per pound for a fully cooked ham (or 130° on meat thermometer).

As an added precaution to keep ham fat away from the barbecue fire, shape a "pan" of double heavy-duty foil loosely around lower half of ham. Sides should be about 4 inches high and should stand away from ham about 1 inch all around. Insert meat thermometer in thick portion of ham.

Set ham on the barbecue, centered over drip pan beneath. For slow heat, keep any draft opening small. Check the ham every half hour; if it begins to brown too quickly, lower heat by making draft openings smaller (but don't completely close them). If drippings accumulate excessively in the pan directly under the ham, remove them with a turkey baster. One hour before ham is done, remove from barbecue, drain off drippings, skin, score, and brush with honey glaze made by combining honey, Worcestershire, mustard, ginger, and pepper. Return to barbecue and brush with glaze about every 15 minutes. When ham is done, it will be easier to slice if you let it stand 15 to 20 minutes. Makes 2 to 3 servings per pound.

CARROT-ASPARAGUS PLATTER

This colorful vegetable platter can be partially prepared ahead. You can cook the carrots a day ahead and refrigerate them; the potato border can be prepared early in the day it is to be served and then refrigerated until the final browning. Makes about 12 servings.

POTATO BORDER. Prepare instant mashed potatoes (amount for 8 servings), adding salt, water, and milk according to directions on package. Add 4 tablespoons butter, 1 tablespoon instant minced onion, and 2 eggs, beating until thoroughly blended. Spoon this mixture with teaspoon or press through cake decorator onto a large ovenproof platter or plank (about 18 by 24 inches) to make the decorative border for the carrots and asparagus; refrigerate until ready to cook vegetables.

While you glaze carrots and cook asparagus, brown potato border in a 375° oven for about 10 minutes. Arrange hot vegetables within the borders.

GLAZED GINGERED CARROTS. In a small amount of water cook 4 cups carrots (about 2 pounds), cut in chunks, until almost tender, 12 to 15 minutes. In a saucepan melt 3 tablespoons butter and stir in 2 tablespoons brown sugar, 1 tablespoon instant minced onion, ½ teaspoon ground ginger, ¼ teaspoon salt, and ⅛ teaspoon pepper.

Add carrots and stir carefully to coat them completely with the mixture. Turn carrots in pan over medium heat, until glazed and thoroughly heated, about 5 minutes. Arrange in center of platter.

BUTTERED PARMESAN ASPARAGUS. Cook 4 pounds fresh asparagus in a small amount of water until tender, about 10 minutes. Drain and season with 1 tablespoon butter, ½ teaspoon salt, and ⅛ teaspoon pepper. Arrange on both sides of carrots on platter and sprinkle with 2 tablespoons grated Parmesan cheese.

GRAPEFRUIT-AVOCADO SALAD

The grapefruit for this salad can be prepared ahead; cover it with plastic film and refrigerate until you are ready to assemble the salad.

1	pink grapefruit
1½	large heads romaine lettuce
1	avocado
	French dressing

Cut away peel—including all the white membrane—from grapefruit; remove the sections. Shred lettuce and pile into salad bowl. Top with grapefruit. Peel and slice avocado and arrange on salad. Add your favorite French dressing. Makes 12 servings.

Tahitian Party

BUFFET FOR TWELVE TO SIXTEEN PEOPLE

ICED WINE PUNCH

CURRIED PRAWNS WITH STEAMED RICE

CONDIMENT CHICKEN SALAD WITH AVOCADO

HOT FRENCH BREAD SLICES

FRUIT PÖE WITH COCONUT CREAM

TAHITIAN COFFEE WITH COCONUT MILK

You'll enjoy a Tahitian feast scaled down to dinner-party size. It is a party that's easy to stage—no long-range planning or hours of food preparation. Yet the island dishes are sumptuous. French influence has given Tahiti perhaps the most highly refined cuisine of all the South Pacific islands. Although this is a Tahitian feast, it is not a typical Tamaaraa—a formidable affair with vast quantities of food, requiring days of preparation.

Decorating. Here are some ideas for decorating.

The pareu *cloth (par-a-oo)* plays an important part in the Tahitian way of life. It is colored cotton with a bold contrasting flower or fern pattern in white. Tahitians use the cloth as a house decoration, for curtains, to cover pillows and cushions, as a tablecloth. Men and women use it as a garment (the men wind it around the waist; women wear it sarong-style).

Ferns, broad green leaves, and flowers are useful props for your Tahitian decor. Use sword ferns or broad-leafed cannas or buy ti leaves from your florist.

Bamboo, reed, and straw, in any form, lend a tropical touch. You can use baskets or trays as serving containers, filled with fruits and flowers, or as a lamp shield. Or pin a piece of straw matting on your wall.

Tropical fruits are useful—decorate with them wherever you wish.

Ornaments from the sea—you can use seashells, starfish, fish netting, imitation coral and seaweed, colored glass float balls.

Couronnes. Tahitian men and women wear headbands of ferns and flowers, called couronnes *(cor-o-nas).* You can make them yourself for the guests, but it's more fun to have the makings on hand and let the guests create their own. Here are directions:

Select fairly sturdy leaves (sword fern or stephanotis would be fine). Using a heavy needle and thread, fasten the stem and tip of a leaf together to form a crown of the correct head size. (You may have to sew several leaves together to get enough length.) Then sew flowers, here and there, onto the fern band.

WHITE WINE PUNCH

Slices of fresh citrus fruits garnish this flavorful punch. Start making it a day before the party to let flavors mingle. Leave the split vanilla bean in the punch when you serve it.

1   *medium-sized pineapple, peeled and cut into fine chunks*
½   *cup brown sugar, firmly packed*
½   *whole nutmeg, grated*
1   *vanilla bean, slit in half lengthwise*
    Sections of 2 grapefruits
    Sections of 2 oranges
    Zest (outer peel) of 1 lime
    Juice of 2 limes
1   *bottle (4/5 qt.) of chilled dry white wine*
6   *cups fruit juice (orange, pineapple, grapefruit, or a combination)*

The day before the party, place in a large bowl or pitcher the pineapple, brown sugar, nutmeg, and vanilla bean. Mix and cover. Place in a cool place (not in refrigerator), and allow to stand 12 to 24 hours.

To serve, add the grapefruit and orange sections. Twist strips of lime zest to extract oil and drop into punch. Add lime juice, wine, and fruit juice. Pour over ice in a large punch bowl. Makes about 2½ quarts.

CURRIED PRAWNS

Large Baja California prawns make a very good substitute for the fresh-water prawns found in Tahitian waters. Serve them over fluffy steamed rice, so the seasoned butter and wine cooking juices can be enjoyed also.

To eat, pick up prawns in your fingers, suck out the juices, then break off the shell and eat the meat with fingers or with a fork.

2	large onions, chopped fine
6	tablespoons melted butter
5	to 6 pounds (about 7 dozen) large prawns, washed and drained
6	cloves garlic, minced or mashed
4	to 5 teaspoons curry powder
1	cup sweet Sauterne
½	cup freshly chopped parsley
	About 8 cups steamed, hot rice

Sauté onions in melted butter until yellow. Add prawns, then garlic and curry. Stir well. Add wine. Cover and cook over very low heat 15 minutes. Just before serving, sprinkle with the freshly chopped parsley. Serve the curried prawns with fluffy rice. Makes 12 servings.

CONDIMENT CHICKEN SALAD WITH AVOCADO

This unusual chicken salad is rich with chicken meat and curry condiments. Mound the salad on a big bed of salad greens and garnish with thick slices of ripe avocado.

To plump the raisins, let them stand in white wine a few hours before making the salad.

1½	cups mayonnaise
1	cup raisins
1	cup salted peanuts
1	cup mango chutney, cut into slivers
1	cup flaked coconut
2	pounds cooked chicken meat, diced coarsely
2	cups diagonally sliced ripe bananas
	Salt and pepper to taste
	Salad greens
	Avocado slices
	Additional sliced bananas
	Lemon juice

Mix together the mayonnaise, raisins, peanuts, chutney, and coconut. Toss with chicken meat. Gently combine with sliced bananas. Season with salt and pepper.

Mound into large salad bowl or on a platter lined with shredded lettuce and lettuce leaves. Garnish with slices of avocado and banana, which you have dipped into lemon juice. Makes 12 servings.

FRESH FRUIT POË

Tahitians make many varieties of poë desserts. (Tahitians would make it with arrowroot starch rather than cornstarch.) The chilled coconut cream poured over the top in this version is made of coconut milk and evaporated milk.

	About 2 papayas and 1 fresh pineapple (to make 4 cups puréed fresh fruit)
2	cups cornstarch
2	cups sugar
	Grated fresh coconut (or packaged flaked coconut)
1	pint (2 cups) chilled coconut milk (purchased frozen)
2	cups chilled evaporated milk

Peel papayas and remove seeds; peel and core pineapple. Purée in blender or force through food mill to make 4 cups puréed fruit. Stir in cornstarch and sugar. Turn into greased and floured baking pan (8 by 10 inches). Bake in a 350° oven for an hour or until set and caramelized at corners. Allow to cool in pan a few minutes. Cut into 1-inch squares. Lift onto shallow tray or into serving bowl. Sprinkle with grated coconut. For coconut cream topping, combine coconut milk and evaporated milk and pour over warm cubes of poë. Makes 12 servings.

TAHITIAN COFFEE WITH COCONUT MILK

Heat 2 cups milk until a film forms on top. Add 1 can (4 oz.) or 1 cup flaked coconut and 2 tablespoons sugar. Cover and allow to stand in the refrigerator overnight. Strain milk and reheat slowly. Combine milk with 2 cups freshly brewed strong, hot coffee. Serve with a topping of toasted coconut, if desired. Makes 6 coffee-cup servings.

(*Note: This coffee can also be served chilled. Pour into brandy snifters or glass tumblers and serve as an afternoon refreshment.*)

Nouveau Riche Hamburgers

FOR TWELVE TO TWENTY-FOUR PEOPLE

BURGUNDY BURGERS WITH ROQUEFORT

HAMBURGER BUNS WITH SESAME SEED

ELEGANT ONIONS

BUTTER LETTUCE

BEEFSTEAK TOMATOES

FRENCH CHAMPAGNE MUSTARD

When "just plain folks" suddenly come into a lot of money, they may begin to surround themselves with all sorts of elegant trappings. But their simple origins are difficult to disguise. That's why we call these "new rich" hamburgers. They are decked out with fancy trimmings, ready for a sophisticated party, but no one is really fooled.

You dress up the hamburgers with wine and cheese, broil, and place on freshly home-baked buns, a real delicacy. Top them with dill-and-parsley-flecked onion slivers, leaves of tender butter lettuce, and thick slices of choice tomatoes. Then spread with imported mustard made with Champagne, bought at a gourmet food shop.

As special as these hamburgers sound, they are very practical to prepare. The meat patties can be shaped and marinated ahead. The buns may be frozen after baking, days in advance if you wish. The method of preparing the onions takes away some of the strong flavor and keeps them looking good long after they have been sliced. Butter lettuce leaves are just the right size to fit hamburger buns. Beefsteak tomatoes are solid, not juicy, so these elegant burgers can be tidily munched by the most refined.

BURGUNDY BURGERS WITH ROQUEFORT

8	pounds ground beef chuck
1	cup chopped parsley
1	cup chopped green onion
2½	tablespoons salt
½	teaspoon pepper
1	bottle (4/5 quart) dry red wine
24	squares Roquefort or blue cheese (about 12 oz.)

Mix together the ground chuck, parsley, and the green onion; season with salt and pepper. Shape into

24 patties, making a depression in the center of each one. Place in a shallow pan and pour wine over patties, pouring into the depressions. Chill 2 hours or longer. Remove meat patties from marinade and broil over medium hot coals, for 8 to 10 minutes for medium rare. Place a small square of Roquefort or blue cheese on each meat patty just before serving so it will melt slightly.

HAMBURGER BUNS

Warm homemade buns, topped with seeds (poppy, celery, caraway, sesame), dried onion flakes, or just left plain, are a special treat for a hamburger supper. Buns are shaped and baked in small foil pans; they may be made ahead and frozen.

2	packages yeast, active dry or compressed
½	cup warm water (lukewarm for compressed yeast)
2	cups milk, scalded and cooled
1	cup (½ lb.) butter or margarine, melted and cooled
¼	cup sugar
4	teaspoons salt
4	eggs, slightly beaten
9½	cups unsifted all-purpose flour
1	egg
1	teaspoon water
	Sesame, celery, caraway, or poppy seeds or dried onion flakes

Dissolve yeast in the ½ cup warm water. Combine milk, butter, sugar, salt, the 4 eggs, and 4 cups of the flour in a large bowl. Beat well with an electric mixer about 2 minutes.

Beat in remaining flour by hand to make a soft dough. Turn out on a lightly floured board and knead until smooth and elastic, about 10 minutes. Place dough in a greased bowl, cover, and let rise in a warm place until doubled in bulk, about 1½ hours. Then punch dough down and shape it.

Lightly grease 24 foil pans, each about 4 inches in diameter. Form smooth-topped balls of dough about 2 inches in diameter. Place dough in pans, pressing to flatten. Beat the 1 egg with the 1 teaspoon water; brush buns. Sprinkle each with 1 teaspoon seeds or onion flakes. Set pans on baking sheets; let dough rise in warm place until almost doubled in bulk, about 30 minutes. Bake in a 375° oven for 12 to 15 minutes, or until lightly browned. Cool 5 minutes, then turn out on racks. Wrap when cool; freeze if you wish. Makes about 24 buns.

ELEGANT ONIONS

Slice 4 large sweet onions in half lengthwise, then slice thinly, lengthwise. Sprinkle generously with salt, then let stand 15 minutes. Squeeze onions in hands until limp, rinse well to remove salt, then mix them with ½ cup chopped parsley and ½ teaspoon dill weed (optional).

Oriental Meal Cooked at the Table

FOR FOUR PEOPLE

JAPANESE CUCUMBER SALAD

ALTERNATE 1: CASHEW CHICKEN

ALTERNATE 2: JAVANESE SATÉS

HOT STEAMED RICE

GINGER ICE CREAM SUNDAES

Guests enjoy an intimate supper party when the main dish is cooked right at the table. But the hostess probably enjoys it most, because she need not spend any of her time in the kitchen.

Such a meal seems to be most successful when the number of diners is limited to four, or six at most.

With the preceding menu, you have a choice of main dishes, depending on your tastes and the method of cooking you prefer.

The Cashew Chicken takes only about 5 minutes to cook in an electric frying pan. If you have a table-size hibachi, you may prefer the Javanese Satés, which will cook in about 10 minutes each.

Serve the marinated cucumber salads first, in individual bowls, to whet the guests' appetites while the main dish is cooking.

The candied ginger sauce for the ice cream is also made ahead; it can be served either warm or chilled. Before dinner time, all you have to do is cook the rice.

JAPANESE CUCUMBER SALAD

This salad contains no salad oil—just white vinegar, a little sugar, salt, and slivered fresh ginger root. It can well accompany many types of roast meats, curries, or dishes with an Oriental or tropical flavor.

    2   large cucumbers
    ⅓   cup white vinegar
    4   teaspoons sugar
    1   teaspoon salt
    2   slices fresh ginger, finely chopped or
          slivered

Cut cucumbers in half lengthwise and remove any large seeds. Slice crosswise into very thin slices. Marinate in a mixture of the vinegar, sugar, salt, and ginger. Chill in the marinade an hour or longer. (To carry salad to a picnic, take it in the marinade, perhaps in a vacuum bottle.) Makes 4 to 6 servings.

CASHEW CHICKEN

This Chinese-style stir-fry dish takes only 5 minutes of cooking in an electric frying pan, making it an ideal cook-at-the-table entrée. Arrange the vegetables on a tray and put the sauce ingredients in pitchers to make sure the preparation moves speedily.

3	whole chicken breasts, split
½	pound Chinese (edible pod) peas or 2 pkgs. frozen pods, partially thawed
½	pound mushrooms
4	green onions
1	can (15 oz.) bamboo shoots
1	tablespoon chicken stock base and 1 cup water
¼	cup soy sauce
2	tablespoons cornstarch
½	teaspoon each sugar and salt
4	tablespoons salad or peanut oil
1	package (4 oz.) cashew nuts

Bone chicken breasts and remove skin. Slice horizontally in ⅛-inch-thick slices, then cut in 1-inch squares. Arrange on a tray. Remove the ends and strings from the Chinese peas. Wash and slice mushrooms. Cut the green part of the onions into 1-inch lengths and then slash both ends several times making small fans; slice the white part ¼ inch thick. Drain bamboo shoots and slice. Arrange all the vegetables on the tray in individual piles.

Pour chicken stock into a small pitcher. Mix together soy with cornstarch, sugar, and salt; pour into a small pitcher. Place oil and nuts in containers. Arrange at the table with electric frying pan.

To cook, heat 1 tablespoon oil over moderate heat (350°), add nuts all at once, and cook 1 minute, shaking pan, until lightly toasted; remove from pan and set aside. Add remaining oil to pan, add chicken, and cook quickly, turning, until it turns opaque. Add Chinese peas and mushrooms; pour in stock, cover, and simmer 2 minutes.

Add bamboo shoots. Stir the soy mixture into the pan juices, and cook until sauce is thickened, stirring constantly; then simmer 1 minute uncovered. Mix in the green onions. Sprinkle with nuts. Makes 4 servings.

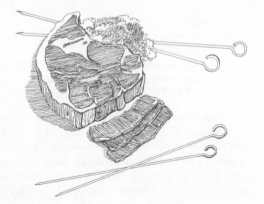

JAVANESE SATÉS

A table hibachi handles the barbecuing of interlaced steak strips and tropical fruits for this succulent Indonesian kebab. Guests spoon the assorted condiments into mounds on their dinner plates and intermingle them with both beef and fruits.

½	cup sesame seed
1½	pounds top round steak, sliced ¾ inch thick
⅓	cup soy sauce
3	tablespoons Sherry
2	tablespoons salad oil
½	cup finely chopped onion
½	teaspoon ground ginger
3	cloves garlic, minced
1	papaya or small cantaloupe
4	small bananas
1	small pineapple
½	cup Major Grey chutney
	Condiments: chutney, toasted coconut, lime wedges, yogurt

Toast sesame seed in a 350° oven 10 minutes; pulverize in a blender until very fine or crush in a mortar and pestle; place in a small bowl. Slice round steak into four long strips, each about ¾ inch thick. Mix together the soy, Sherry, oil, onion, ginger, and garlic, and let meat marinate for 30 minutes. Thread on skewers in serpentine fashion (weave in and out on strip of meat lengthwise).

Peel papaya, halve, and remove seeds; cut in sixths. Peel back a 1-inch strip on each banana. Peel pineapple, halve, and cut in long slices. Purée chutney in a blender or chop finely; brush on fruit. Arrange fruit and meat on tray at table.

To cook, barbecue meat over hot coals, turning once (allow about 5 minutes to a side, or until meat is browned). Sprinkle lightly with toasted sesame seed. Meanwhile, skewer fruit lengthwise with bamboo sticks; place on barbecue along with meat (banana should have peeled side down) to heat through and brown slightly. Pass bowls of condiments. Makes 4 servings.

GINGER SUNDAES

To make sauce, combine 2 cups sugar, ¼ teaspoon cream of tartar, and 1 cup water in a pan. Bring to a boil; simmer about 6 minutes or until temperature reaches 232° on a candy thermometer (syrup spins 2-inch thread when dropped from spoon). Cool about 10 minutes. Put 7 pieces preserved ginger and 1 tablespoon *each* lemon juice and syrup from ginger into blender; whirl smooth. Blend in ¼ cup whipping cream or ice cream, cooled syrup, and 1 drop yellow food coloring. Serve warm or chilled over vanilla ice cream. Top with fresh fruit, nuts, or chopped candied ginger, if you wish. Makes 4 servings.

Wintertime Buffet

FOR TEN PEOPLE

CREAM OF BROCCOLI SOUP

COLD SLICED TONGUE AND BEEF TENDERLOIN

PARSLEY-BUTTERED NEW POTATOES

SCALLOPED MUSHROOMS

GREEN SALAD

PUMPKIN ICE CREAM PIE
Recipe on page 56

This partly cold, partly hot buffet is a good choice for winter—and especially holiday—entertaining. Many of the foods can be prepared ahead, so you can easily organize your menu around the holiday rush.

CREAM OF BROCCOLI SOUP

Serve the soup in pottery mugs, floating a pretzel in each. Pass them to guests in the living room before you leave to make last-minute dinner preparations in the kitchen. You can prepare the soup up to a day ahead.

2	packages (10 oz. each) frozen chopped broccoli, thawed
¼	cup chopped onion
2	cups regular strength chicken broth
2	tablespoons butter
1	tablespoon flour
2	teaspoons salt
⅛	teaspoon mace
	Dash pepper
2	cups half-and-half (light cream)

In a medium-sized pan, combine broccoli, onion, and chicken broth; bring to a boil. Simmer for about 10 minutes, or until broccoli is tender. Whirl broccoli mixture in blender until very smooth, or press through a food mill or wire strainer. Melt the butter in a pan; add flour, salt, mace, and pepper, stirring until smooth. Slowly stir in half-and-half, then add broccoli purée. Cook over medium heat, stirring often, until soup bubbles. If soup is made ahead, cool and refrigerate. Serve hot. Makes 10 to 12 servings of ½ cup each.

COLD SLICED TONGUE AND BEEF TENDERLOIN

A horseradish sauce complements two kinds of chilled cooked meat in this recipe. The sliced tongue and beef tenderloin are served together on a tray, with cherry tomatoes, stuffed green olives, and marinated artichoke hearts to add touches of color.

2½	to 3-pound fresh beef tongue
1	tablespoon salt
8	to 10 whole allspice
1	small onion, sliced
	Cold water
4	to 6-pound beef tenderloin
¼	cup butter
1	clove garlic, minced
	Cherry tomatoes
	Stuffed green olives
	Marinated artichoke hearts

Place beef tongue in a deep pan with salt, allspice, onion, and water to cover. Bring water to a boil, then reduce heat and simmer until the tongue is fork-tender. (Allow about 1 hour per pound.) Cool tongue in liquid, remove, and cut off the bones and gristle at the thick end. Slit the skin on the underside, starting at the thick end; loosen the skin with a sharp paring knife, then peel and pull it off, working from the thick end to the tip. Chill and slice thinly.

Remove surface fat and connective tissue from the beef tenderloin; place the meat on a rack in a roasting pan. Tuck the narrow end of the tenderloin under to make a uniform thickness. Melt butter and blend with garlic; brush meat with the butter mixture. Roast the tenderloin in a 450° oven for 30 minutes for rare meat or 40 minutes for medium; baste occasionally

with garlic butter. Chill and slice meat thinly to serve.

Arrange cold sliced meats on a large wooden tray. Alternate cherry tomatoes, stuffed green olives, and marinated artichoke hearts on wooden picks for garnish. Serve with Fluffy Horseradish Sauce. Makes 10 to 12 servings.

FLUFFY HORSERADISH SAUCE. Whip 1 cup heavy cream until stiff; fold in 3 tablespoons prepared horseradish, 2 teaspoons sugar, and 1 teaspoon lemon juice. Chill in serving bowl for several hours; sprinkle with chopped chives just before serving. Makes about 2 cups.

SCALLOPED MUSHROOMS

Toasty buttered bread crumbs top this mushroom casserole, which can be assembled ahead of time to be baked just before dinner.

1½   *pounds fresh mushrooms, washed, drained, and sliced*
3   *cups soft French bread crumbs (fresh bread whirled in blender)*
¾   *cup butter, melted*
   Salt and pepper
½   *cup dry white wine*

Place about a third of the mushrooms in a buttered 2-quart baking dish; cover with about a third of the bread crumbs, and drizzle about a third of the butter over the crumbs. Sprinkle with salt and pepper. For the top layer, cover with remaining mushrooms; sprinkle them with salt and pepper, and pour wine over all. Cover and bake in a 325° oven for about 35 minutes. Mix remaining butter and crumbs, and spoon over mushrooms. Bake uncovered 10 more minutes, or until crumbs are toasted. Makes about 12 servings.

COOKING WITH WINE

Cooking with wine is easy if you use this cook book. The recipes tell just what quantities and types to use; you merely measure as you would any other ingredient. Wines for cooking purposes should be of fairly good quality—wines you'd enjoy drinking for their own sake.

In the case of an appetizer or dessert wine, the recipe specifies the exact kind of Vermouth, Sherry, or Port. Often a "dry white" or "dry red" wine is called for. In the case of white wines, you may use any non-sweet table wine such as Chablis, dry Sauterne, or Rhine types. Even dry Vermouth, which is an herb-flavored white wine, may be substituted in some recipes, particularly in dishes with herb seasoning or where a small quantity of wine is specified. A dry red wine may be either the Burgundy or Claret types, or Italian reds.

You may prefer to buy half-bottles of the table wines which are perishable. Larger opened bottles may be preserved by refrigeration. Frequently it is convenient to use some of the same table wine that will be served with dinner in preparing the food; this helps avoid leftover wine. Appetizer and dessert wines have a higher alcohol content and therefore are more resistant to spoilage. They may be stored for several months after opening.

Wine used in cooking may serve several purposes. A few spoonfuls will point up or blend flavors, yet may remain unnoticed, just as a little lemon juice or garlic often is. If you have no wine on hand, such a small quantity can probably be omitted without changing the dish to any important extent. Larger quantities, usually called for by the cupful, contribute a definite flavor, and wine must be used if the dish is to taste as it should. Because wine also is a good tenderizer, it is useful in meat cookery; marinating or long simmering is necessary to take advantage of this characteristic. The dessert wines act much the way an extract does—several spoonfuls will impart a definite and identifiable flavor.

In experimenting with wine cookery, use a cautious approach as you would if trying new herbs or spices. Add a small amount and taste. However, wine added to cooking food does behave differently from herbs and spices, which may increase in pungency as the heat brings out their flavor. The alcohol in wine evaporates even below the boiling point, and heat seems to mellow the remaining flavor. Thus the taste will become subtler the longer cooking goes on, unless the liquid is reduced to such an extent that the wine in it is more concentrated.

When marinating foods in wine, be sure to use non-metallic containers. Utensils used for cooking foods with wine may be metal. In either case, cover the vessel to prevent evaporation of the essence.

Adding wine to foods is no more mysterious than adding salt. It is helpful to have a recipe which tells an exact amount of salt to use, but even a relatively inexperienced cook soon learns how to salt most foods without measuring. With a little practice the same kind of feel for adding wine can be acquired. Although over-salting can ruin a dish, "over-wining" is a seldom occurrence—wine does not need such precise measuring.

Champagne Party

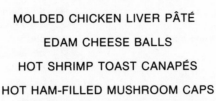

MOLDED CHICKEN LIVER PÂTÉ

EDAM CHEESE BALLS

HOT SHRIMP TOAST CANAPÉS

HOT HAM-FILLED MUSHROOM CAPS

FRESH PAPAYA OR MELON AND PROSCIUTTO

CELERY OR FENNEL AND GIANT RIPE OLIVES IN ICE RING

CHAMPAGNE OR CHAMPAGNE FRUIT PUNCH

The food for a Champagne party should be delicate, bite-size, and unusually attractive. One or more kinds of hot tidbits passed on trays are particularly welcome. Presenting such a party without catering or serving help is not easy, but it is possible to offer this selection of appetizers with no more than one member of the family being away briefly for last-minute attention to the hot foods.

The molded pâté topped with amber aspic, can be made a day ahead. With it serve small, thin triangles of dark bread, and provide butter knives for spreading. Cut the top off a red Edam cheese and use a melon-ball cutter to scoop balls out of the center. Smooth out the inside of the waxy red shell, and fill it with the balls; provide toothpicks for spearing the cheese balls. Cut the papaya or melon into bite-size pieces and wrap each piece with a paper-thin sliver of prosciutto or smoked ham; fasten with a pick and arrange on trays.

The mushroom caps may be baked a little ahead, covered, and kept warm. The shrimp canapés can be assembled ahead, broiled briefly just before serving. If you set up a buffet service for the cold items to which guests may help themselves at the beginning of the party, you can slip away after everyone has arrived to complete last-minute cooking and bring in the hot foods.

Use a ring mold to make a ring of ice; you may mold cucumber slices, olives, or leaves of the celery or fennel inside it. Place the ice ring on a platter or in a shallow bowl (sufficient to contain water from melting). Fill the ring with the largest pitted ripe olives you can find. Cut small pieces of celery or fennel in fan shapes and use as garnish for the olives.

Serving punch rather than plain Champagne will be simpler. No one need be occupied with opening bottles and pouring during the party, as guests can help themselves at the punch bowl. The cost is less because the punch also contains still wine and sparkling soda.

MOLDED CHICKEN LIVER PÂTÉ

This is one of those elegant but easy dishes. A mound of shimmering amber gelatin tops this molded pâté, giving it a very special look. Yet the topping is very easily made from canned consommé. The entire dish may be made well ahead of party time, then garnished just before serving.

¼   teaspoon unflavored gelatin
¼   cup each water and condensed consommé
¾   pound chicken livers
     Water
¾   cup soft butter or margarine
3   tablespoons finely chopped onion
1   teaspoon dry mustard
¼   teaspoon each salt, nutmeg, and anchovy
         paste
     Dash each cayenne and cloves
     Lemon slices and watercress for garnish

Soften gelatin in the ¼ cup water. Add consommé and heat, stirring occasionally, until gelatin is completely dissolved. Pour into bottom of a 2½ to 3-cup mold; chill until firm.

Cover livers with water; bring to a boil and simmer for about 20 minutes, or until livers are very tender. Cool slightly in liquid. Drain livers and whirl in blender with butter until mixture is very smooth and fluffy (or press livers through a food mill or strainer; add butter and beat until smooth).

Blend in onion and seasonings. Spread over gelatin in mold, pressing liver mixture in evenly; cover and chill until firm.

Unmold onto serving plate; garnish with lemon slices and watercress. Serve with crisp crackers or buttered rye toast. Makes about 2 cups.

SHRIMP TOAST CANAPÉS

For some strange reason, directions on making this delicious hot canapé can be found in several Chinese recipe books. Perhaps the canapé is of Oriental origin, just as Italian spaghetti is said to be. Who knows?

    1   pound raw shrimp (or 12 oz. shelled and
            deveined frozen shrimp)
    1   green onion, including part of green top
    4   canned water chestnuts
    ½   teaspoon salt
    ¼   teaspoon garlic salt
    ⅛   teaspoon pepper
    1½ teaspoons lemon juice
    1   egg white
    12 thin slices white sandwich bread, crusts
            removed

Shell and devein the raw shrimp, or defrost frozen shrimp. Chop shrimp, onion, and water chestnuts into very fine pieces. Put into a bowl with the salt, garlic salt, pepper, and lemon juice. Mix until well blended. Add unbeaten egg white, mixing it in well. Put bread slices under the broiler until toasted on one side. Turn over and spread untoasted side with the shrimp mixture. This much can be done several hours ahead and appetizers covered with clear plastic film or foil.

Just before serving, brush the top of each sandwich with melted butter and broil until the shrimp topping turns pink. Cut into quarters and serve hot. Makes about 4 dozen canapés.

HAM-FILLED MUSHROOM CAPS

Small stuffed mushroom caps have a natural elegance that can be heightened by placing them in little fluted paper cups, convenient if the mushrooms are to be eaten with the fingers. Very large caps are equally elegant served on a plate for the first course at the table. You can prepare the mushrooms for baking several hours ahead.

    1   pound small whole mushrooms
    ¼   cup butter or margarine
    2   cups ground cooked ham
    ½   cup sour cream
    2   tablespoons minced chives
    6   pitted ripe olives

Remove stems from mushrooms and finely chop enough stems to make 1 cup. (Use remainder for another purpose.) Lightly sauté caps in melted butter and arrange in a buttered baking pan. Mix together ham, sour cream, chives, and the 1 cup chopped mushroom stems; pile inside mushroom caps. Bake in a 350° oven for 10 minutes. Garnish with sliced olive wedges. Makes about 3 dozen.

CHAMPAGNE FRUIT PUNCH

Strawberries garnish this refreshing punch, made with grapefruit soda, Sauterne, and Champagne.

    1   bottle (4/5 qt.) Sauterne, well chilled
    1   bottle (4/5 qt.) Champagne, chilled
    2   bottles (1 qt. each) grapefruit soda,
            well chilled
    2   cups washed, stemmed strawberries

In a punch bowl, mix together until blended the Sauterne, Champagne, and grapefruit soda. Drop in strawberries.

Ladle some of the punch into each punch glass or Champagne glass, and add a strawberry to each serving. Makes 18 to 20 servings.

Italian Fritter Meal

FOR SIX PEOPLE

VEAL INDORATO

TOSSED GREEN SALAD

CRUSTY FRENCH OR ITALIAN BREAD

SPUMONI OR NEAPOLITAN ICE CREAM

Italian fritters are seldom encountered in the numerous Italian restaurants—just in a few long-established places which continue to prepare old-style dishes. Fritters are usually an everyday meal in Italian homes, where the entire meal is made from a large assortment of meats and vegetables, batter fried.

This full-scale production is called Fritto Misto.

VEAL INDORATO

This simple version of *Fritto Misto* features only four ingredients—veal, zucchini, eggplant, and artichoke hearts. Ingredients can be prepared up to an hour ahead, but should be fried just before serving.

3 *boneless veal round steaks (about 1¼ to 1½ lbs.)*
2 *or 3 medium-sized zucchini*
1 *small eggplant*
6 *small artichokes (sometimes called hearts) or about 12 thawed frozen artichoke pieces*
   Vinegar and water
   Salt
   Flour
   Beaten eggs, about 4
   Salad oil or half butter, half salad oil
3 *or 4 lemons, or more*

Prepare for cooking as follows: Trim all membrane and tough connective tissue from veal. Place meat between sheets of waxed paper and pound with a flat-surfaced mallet until the meat is very thin (⅛ to ¼ inch).

Cut zucchini into diagonal slices, each about ⅜ inch thick. Slice eggplant crosswise into pieces about ¼ inch thick, or cut lengthwise into sticks about ⅜ inch thick.

Break tough outer leaves from the artichokes, cut off the top ⅓ (removing all thorns), and trim stem end. Cut in half or quarter each artichoke and place immediately in acid water (1 tablespoon vinegar to each quart water). Drain well to use. Season all foods with salt before cooking.

To cook, turn each piece in the flour and shake off excess, then dip into the beaten egg. Fry over medium-high heat in a wide frying pan containing about ½ inch of hot salad oil (or half butter) until each piece is richly browned. Add more fat as needed, and spoon out the small particles as they accumulate in the pan.

Fry vegetables first, then veal; sauté veal just enough to brown lightly. Place browned pieces on baking sheets lined with paper towels; keep warm in a very slow oven or reheat later in a 350° oven.

Squeeze the juice of at least ½ lemon over each serving. Makes 6 servings.

THE ART OF THE SMALL DINNER PARTY

Of all invitations, those that flatter us most are for small dinner parties. It's a very personal way to entertain, and satisfying to both hosts and guests. Following are some tips that can help you make an intimate dinner party especially successful.

The Setting. A decoration or two in the living room and on the buffet or dining table will make your home look festive. Simple arrangements of flowers, fruits, shells, or other ornaments are often sufficient.

The centerpiece itself is a challenge met in varied and imaginative ways. A large pink shell with a single full-blown garden rose is a striking example. Fruits or vegetables make beautiful and appetizing centerpieces. A golden Casaba melon and clusters of pale green Thompson seedless grapes are handsome in a low, black, free-form bowl. Flowers that float—begonia, camellia, azalea, or rhododendron blossoms—are good choices because you can keep the bouquet low. A few flowers arranged at the bases of candlesticks often suffice and are particularly suitable if your table is small and crowded.

The Serving. The clever hostess plans her menu to require only a few last-minute chores. Certain inevitable tasks like mixing the salad and getting dishes to buffet or table take one away from company long enough.

It's helpful to have chilled plates or bowls from the refrigerator for salad, and hot plates from the oven or warmer for the entrée.

If there is meat or poultry to be carved, let the host do it at the table (if he's willing). The hostess can serve the vegetables, to speed up the process and keep food from getting cold.

Combination Buffet – Sit-Down Dinner. Many hostesses choose a combination plan where guests serve themselves at the buffet, then sit down at a set table. This procedure is easy to handle without outside help, and the guests are comfortably placed at an attractive table.

The partial buffet plan may also work another way. Serve your guests at the dinner table, perhaps having an attractive first course waiting at each place. Then let the dessert be buffet style in the living room. Set up coffee or tea service and a beautiful cake or pastry, with plates. Also place dessert wines or liqueurs and glasses there to pass around later. This helps get guests away from the table and lets those who would like a brief wait after the full meal serve themselves when they are ready.

Picnic for Patrons of the Arts

FOR EIGHT PEOPLE

WIENER BACKHENDL

VEGETABLE-FILLED AVOCADO HALVES

RYE BREAD AND BUTTER SANDWICHES

DRY WHITE WINE OR FRUIT PUNCH

PUNSCHTORTE

VIENNESE COFFEE

The pleasant tradition of picnicking is well adaptable to outdoor concerts and plays. There are many opportunities to attend outdoor performances where you may picnic either before or after.

An easy way to serve, particularly when you are dressed up, is to pack individual boxes for each member of the party. Folding cardboard bakery boxes are good choices. Carry along an extra basket for other picnic essentials.

If your portable cooler is large enough, pack in it the individually boxed meals, chilled wine, and a pressure can of whipped cream. In a basket carry two vacuum bottles of coffee, a corkscrew, paper plates, cups, and napkins. Wrap the wine glasses in extra napkins. Take along a supply of packaged chemically treated papers for wiping sticky fingers (or carry dampened paper towels in a plastic bag), and forks for the salad.

Backhendl is the Viennese variety of fried chicken, in some respects almost as typical of that city's cuisine as Wiener Schnitzel, which it resembles. Crisply crusted, it may be served hot or cold.

Cooked vegetable salads are popular in the German-speaking countries of Europe. This one has a Western touch—the vegetable mixture is heaped into avocado shells. Just before packing the lunches, fill the avocados with vegetables, place them in individual paper containers, and cover with clear plastic film.

Make the cake as much as a day ahead. To prepare, cut in half lengthwise, then cut each half into 6 or 8 slices. Wrap cake slices individually in plastic film and chill until the boxes are packed.

California wine may not resemble the Heuriger, or new wine, of Vienna. But such white wines as chilled Reisling or Traminer will complement this menu nicely. (In areas where wine is inappropriate, substitute a tart fruit punch, kept cool in a vacuum bottle.)

To add a Viennese touch to your coffee, brew it strong and add whipped cream to each cup.

WIENER BACKHENDL

- 2   small (under 2½ lbs.) broiler-fryer chickens, quartered
- 2   teaspoons salt
- ½   cup all-purpose flour
- 4   eggs, beaten
- 2½   cups very fine dry bread crumbs
      Oil for deep frying
      Thin lemon slices
      Cherry tomato slices
      Chopped parsley

Wash and drain broiler-fryers; sprinkle with salt. Coat on all sides with flour, then dip in eggs, and coat with bread crumbs. Place chicken quarters in a single layer in a preheated fry basket. Lower into deep fat preheated to 350°. Fry until well browned and tender, keeping temperature of fat at about 325°, for 8 to 10 minutes. Drain on paper towels. To serve cold, cool chicken, garnish with lemon slices topped with cherry tomato slices and parsley, and wrap in plastic film. Makes 8 servings.

VEGETABLE-FILLED AVOCADOS

You may use frozen mixed vegetables or improvise other combinations from leftovers if you wish.

- 1   package (10 oz.) frozen mixed vegetables
- ¼   cup French dressing
- ¼   cup each finely chopped dill pickle and celery
- 2   teaspoons prepared horseradish
- 2   tablespoons mayonnaise
- 4   small avocados
      Lemon juice

Cook vegetables until barely tender; drain well. Place in a bowl; pour French dressing over them. Cover, refrigerate, and let stand several hours or overnight; drain well.

Fold in dill pickle, celery, horseradish, and mayonnaise until well combined; chill. Halve, pit, but do not peel the avocados; brush cut surfaces with lemon juice to preserve color. Divide vegetable mixture evenly among avocado halves. Makes 8 servings.

PUNSCHTORTE

The tortes of Vienna are notable for variety, richness, and complexity. Using a lemon cake mix as the basis of a Punschtorte simplifies its preparation without sacrificing traditional elements. The lemon, raspberry, and rum flavors of the cake may remind you of a rum *Punsch* (the German spelling).

    1   package (about 1 lb. 3 oz.) lemon cake mix
    2   tablespoons light rum
    ¾   cup seedless raspberry preserves
        Whipped Cream Filling (recipe follows)
        Rum Butter Icing (recipe follows)

Butter and flour sides of a 9 by 13-inch baking pan; line the bottom with brown paper. Prepare lemon cake mix as package directs; bake as directed for a 9 by 13-inch pan. Cool in pan about 10 minutes; turn out onto a rack and cool completely. Cut in half to get 2 rectangles about 9 by 6½ inches each; split halves horizontally to get 4 layers. Sprinkle all surfaces with 2 tablespoons rum.

To assemble the torte, place bottom cake layer on a cutting board; spread with ¼ of the raspberry preserves and then ⅓ of the Whipped Cream Filling (recipe follows). Spread ¼ of the preserves over the cut surface of the next cake layer and place it, preserves side down, over the whipped cream. Repeat with the remaining cake layers, preserves, and ⅓ of the filling. Then put the 2 sets of layers together with remaining filling between.

Trim sides and ends evenly. Spread Rum Butter Icing (recipe follows) over sides and top; reserve part of icing and pipe on in a decorative border of rosettes. Chill for several hours or overnight. Makes 12 to 16 servings.

WHIPPED CREAM FILLING. Soften 1½ teaspoons unflavored gelatin in 2 tablespoons cold water. In a chilled bowl, whip 1½ cups heavy cream until it begins to thicken. Add ⅓ cup sifted powdered sugar, and gradually beat in 3 tablespoons light rum. Slowly pour in gelatin mixture, beating until just stiff enough to hold shape. Use immediately, or cover and chill 2 to 3 hours and beat again before using. Makes about 3 cups.

RUM BUTTER ICING. Cream ½ cup (¼ lb.) soft butter with 1 cup powdered sugar until fluffy. Add ⅓ cup light rum; gradually blend in 4 cups sifted powdered sugar, beating until creamy.

A Waffle Party

ALTERNATE 1: GINGERBREAD WAFFLES
With Ginger Cream
and poached apple slices or applesauce

ALTERNATE 2: ORANGE SPONGE WAFFLES
With berries, Honey Butter, or maple syrup,
and whipped cream or ice cream

Next time you invite friends in for an evening snack, treat them to an old-fashioned waffle party. Serve one or more kinds of waffles with a variety of toppings (see suggestions below). Each guest can concoct his own waffle combination.

Serve with plenty of hot chocolate or coffee.

Along with these gingerbread and orange sponge waffles, you can serve plain waffles made from your favorite recipe or mix. Specific toppings are suggested for each waffle, but you might also serve some of these: sweetened whipped cream, honey, ice cream in a variety of flavors, grated semisweet chocolate, and toasted sliced almonds.

For the waffles you can have the creamed mixture ready and the dry ingredients sifted together in advance. Save the remaining preparations to do while the waffle irons are heating: beat the egg whites, stir the dry ingredients into the creamed mixture, then fold in the egg whites. The batter should not be put together far in advance of baking.

GINGERBREAD WAFFLES

¼ cup butter or margarine
½ cup each dark brown sugar (firmly packed)
    and light molasses
2 eggs, separated
1 cup milk
2 cups all-purpose flour
1½ teaspoons baking powder
1 teaspoon each cinnamon and ground ginger
¼ teaspoon each ground cloves and salt

Cream together the butter or margarine and brown sugar; beat in the molasses, egg yolks, and milk. Sift flour (it isn't necessary to sift instant-type flour), measure, sift with the baking powder, cinnamon, ginger, cloves, and salt. Beat egg whites until soft peaks form. Stir dry ingredients into creamed mixture, then fold in beaten egg whites. Pour batter into preheated waffle baker and bake until lightly browned. Makes about four 6 by 10½-inch waffles.

GINGER CREAM. Whip 1 cup heavy cream and sweeten with 2 teaspoons sugar; fold in 2 tablespoons finely chopped crystallized ginger.

ORANGE SPONGE WAFFLES

4 eggs, separated
⅔ cup sugar
¼ cup milk
2 teaspoons grated orange peel
1 cup all-purpose flour
½ teaspoon salt
2 tablespoons sugar

Beat egg yolks with the ⅔ cup sugar until thick and pale yellow; beat in the milk and orange peel. Sift flour (don't sift instant-type flour), measure, sift with the salt. Beat egg whites until soft peaks form; gradually beat in the 2 tablespoons sugar until mixture is glossy. Fold egg yolk mixture and flour into beaten egg whites. Spoon batter into preheated waffle baker and bake until lightly browned. Makes four 6 by 10½-inch waffles.

HONEY BUTTER. Beat ½ cup softened butter or margarine until creamy; gradually beat in ¼ cup honey.

Spanish Paella

FOR EIGHT PEOPLE

SPANISH OLIVES, SALTED ROASTED ALMONDS, PICKLED ARTICHOKES

STUFFED EGGS

PAELLA

MIXED LETTUCES WITH OIL AND VINEGAR

NATILLUS

Paella ("pah-ey-yuh") is the classic Spanish potpourri of saffron-flavored rice cooked with meats and seafoods—a liberal definition, perhaps, but one that suggests the extraor-dinary variety of combinations typical of this hearty meal-in-one-dish.

The Spanish cook it in a special wide, shallow frying

pan called a paella pan, available in kitchenware shops in the larger cities here. A frying pan 14 inches or more in diameter can also be used; otherwise brown the meats in two medium-sized frying pans, then blend all together in a big, deeper pan. The least tidy (and most aromatic) part of the cooking can be done the day before.

Serve the olives, nuts, artichokes, and eggs as appetizers with dry Sherry.

The custard and meringues for the Natillus may be prepared ahead, but the dessert should not be assembled more than 4 hours before serving time.

PAELLA

Have your meatman cut up the chicken as usual, then chop each piece into smaller sections. Free the cooked lobster meat from the shell and then put it back in place to serve. The shrimp are cooked in their shells; guests peel them to eat.

2	to 4 tablespoons olive oil or salad oil
4	large onions, chopped
1	pound lean, boneless pork, cut in ¾-inch cubes
3	pound broiler-fryer chicken, cut in about 2-inch pieces
	About 2 teaspoons salt
2	medium-sized (about 6 oz. total) mildly seasoned chorizos, casings removed
1	large peeled, seeded, and diced tomato
1½	cups uncooked long grain rice
5½	to 6 cups chicken broth (canned or freshly made)
1/16	teaspoon saffron
1½	pounds large shrimp, deveined and unshelled (see directions below)
4	small (about ½ lb. each) rock lobster tails, split lengthwise
1	can (4 oz.) whole pimientos, thickly sliced
	About ½ cup minced parsley

Heat 2 tablespoons of the oil in a very wide frying pan (or 2 regular-sized pans) and add onions; cook over high heat, stirring, until soft and lightly browned. Push onions to one side of the pan. Sprinkle pork and chicken with about 1½ teaspoons of salt. Brown pork on all sides over high heat, then push to one side of the pan. Scrape free the accumulating browned particles continuously. Add chicken to pan, a few pieces at a time to avoid crowding, and as pieces become well browned remove to a small bowl.

Pour remaining oil into pan if needed. Crumble chorizos in pan, add tomato and rice, and continue cooking over high heat, stirring, until rice is lightly toasted. Return chicken and pork to cooked mixture. (At this point you can cool the mixture and refrigerate, covered, overnight. Reheat to use.)

Mix 4 cups of the chicken broth and saffron into the hot rice mixture. Cook rapidly, stirring, for 10 minutes. Then add the shrimp and lobster (thawed if frozen) and an additional 1½ cups broth. Cook rapidly, uncovered and stirring frequently, for about 20 minutes more or until rice is tender (add more broth if needed to prevent sticking).

Carefully fold in pimiento, ½ cup parsley, and salt to taste. Keep paella warm up to 45 minutes in a 300° oven before serving. Arrange shellfish over rice and sprinkle with more parsley. Makes 8 servings.

Note: To devein shrimp without shelling, insert a thin wooden or metal skewer into the back of each shrimp just below the vein and gently pull to surface; repeat several times as required.

NATILLUS

This variation of Spanish Natillus or French Floating Island (Oeufs à la Neige) has caramel syrup decoratively dribbled over the meringue floating in custard. The caramel hardens into crunchy candy.

You can prepare the custard up to a day ahead and bake the meringues as much as 8 hours before serving. If you make the dessert ahead, top with syrup no more than 4 hours ahead so it will be crisp.

6	eggs
⅛	teaspoon each salt and cream of tartar
1	cup plus 2 tablespoons sugar
1½	cups half-and-half (light cream)
1½	cups milk
	Grated peel of 1 lemon
2	teaspoons vanilla

Separate 3 of the eggs. Beat the 3 egg whites until foamy, add salt and cream of tartar, and beat until stiff, then gradually beat in 6 tablespoons sugar. Pour 1 inch of hot water into a 9 by 13-inch baking pan; spoon meringue in 6 balls onto water. Place in a 425° oven; bake for 8 minutes, or until lightly browned. Remove from oven. Holding meringues with spatula, drain off water. Let stand at room temperature.

Pour half-and-half and milk into the top of a double boiler, place over hot water, and heat until scalded. Beat remaining 3 whole eggs and the 3 egg yolks until light; gradually beat in ½ cup of remaining sugar. Pour hot milk into egg mixture, return to top of double boiler, and add grated lemon peel. Stirring constantly, cook until custard coats the spoon in a thick, velvety, opaque layer. Stir in vanilla. Immediately remove from heat and place in a pan of cold water to cool. When cool, pour into a serving bowl or individual dessert bowls, cover, and chill.

When ready to serve, gently spoon the meringues onto the custard. Pour remaining ¼ cup sugar into a heavy saucepan and place over moderate heat just until sugar turns amber and melts into a syrup (shake pan frequently to prevent scorching). Slowly pour hot sugar syrup over custard and meringues. Serve at once or hold up to 4 hours. Makes 6 servings.

A GUIDE TO SERVING CHEESES

Probably as many as 100 cheeses are now sold in America. Following is a guide to about 65 of the most widely available kinds.

Hard Grating Cheeses. A few very hard cheeses are almost always grated for cooked dishes or for sprinkling on pastas and salads. Most familiar are sharp, piquant Romano, Parmesan, and dry Monterey Jack. Sapsago, a small cone-shaped cheese flavored and colored sage green with powdered clover leaves, is specified in a few recipes.

Cheddar and Cheddar Types. These range in flavor from mild to very sharp and in color from cream to deep yellow-orange. Cheddar originated in England, but most sold in this country is American-made, sometimes called American cheese or by a trade name. Several English Cheddar types—cream-colored, mild Caerphilly and crumbly, medium-sharp Cheshire—are now imported.

Full-Flavored, Firm Cheeses. Some of these compact cheeses have a very distinctive tang which leaves a bit of an aftertaste. Most pronounced is Port Salut or the Danish version of this cheese, Esrom. Tilsit (Danish Havarti), Beer Kaese, Münster, and mellow Brick are somewhat less assertive in flavor in varying degrees.

Of entirely different character, Greek Kasera (Kasseri) and American Fontinella resemble Parmesan but are soft enough to be sliced. If aged, they become hard enough for grating.

Swiss and Gruyère Types. Several cheeses have holes or "eyes" caused by certain bacteria, which also contribute a characteristic nutty flavor. Swiss with large holes and Gruyère with smaller ones are the best-known. Others similar are French Emmental, Danish Emmenthaler, and Danish Samsoe.

Mild Cheeses (Firm to Semi-Soft). Smooth Gouda and Edam are much alike in their nutlike flavor, yellow coloring, spherical shape, and red wax coating.

American Chantelle, Italian Fontina, and several Danish cheeses (Tybo, Elbo, Danbo, and a Fontina type) all have similar oily-rich texture.

White Monterey Jack and Teleme are more bland, slightly salty, and characterized by a somewhat elastic texture. Teleme softens as it ripens.

An even more elastic, resilient texture is shared by three Italian cheeses generally used for cooking because of their melting qualities. Pale yellow Mozzarella is the pizza cheese (Caciocavallo is similarly used). Smoky Provolone, well-aged, is excellent for appetizers.

Several cheeses with creamy, smooth texture and pleasant, light flavor have been recently introduced in Western America. Danish St. Paulin resembles Italian Bel Paese, which has been widely distributed for some time. Other relative newcomers are Pont L'Eveque with ochre crust,

mildly pungent Reblochon, and smooth Bonbel, usually purchased in a sphere coated with yellow paraffin.

Blue-Veined Cheeses. Genuine Roquefort, made only in France, is sharp and very crumbly when cool. Italian Gorgonzola is richer, less sharp, and more pungent; the fine English Stilton tends to be more restrained. Others streaked with blue or greenish mold are called "blue" in America or "bleu" in France. Such Danish cheeses may be labeled Danablu, Danish blue, or Mycella (which resembles Gorgonzola).

Pungent Ripened Cheeses with Edible Crusts. Soft-crusted with very creamy interior when ripe, these range from very strong to subtle (all a variation on what might be described as an earthy or mushroom-like flavor).

Infamous Limburger can scent a whole room. Liederkranz is similar, but less powerful and odoriferous.

Next down the potency scale is Camembert, which turns to a velvety cream when perfectly ripe; Brie is similar, but slightly more delicate.

Most mild are Neufchâtel and California-made Breakfast Cheese. When unripe, they resemble cream cheese, but become more and more zesty as they mature.

All these cheeses are relatively mild when young and increase in potency with the ripening process.

Buttery, Creamy Cheeses. Several very light French cheeses, somewhat like American cream cheese but more buttery, are now available at a few cheese shops. Delectable Boursault, Gervais, and Boursin are especially fine for dessert, served with fruit.

Danish white cream cheese also is becoming more widely distributed, often labeled Ballet or Castello.

Specialty and Flavored Cheeses. Some are so unique they are best described individually rather than categorized.

Kuminost is much like Jack, but is seasoned with cumin and flecked with caraway seeds. Dutch Leyden, also spiced with these seeds plus cloves, has a Cheddar-like color and texture.

Rich, white French Le Grappe is encrusted with the seeds and skins remaining after grapes are pressed for wine—this imparts a certain savoriness and may be eaten by those who like the crunchiness.

Two soft French types—Gourmandise and Nec Plus Ultra—are spiked with kirsch (cherry brandy) or walnut flavoring. (La Beau Pasteur is similar but unflavored.)

Norwegian Gjetost (pronounced "yeet-ost") is a very solid, caramel-flavored, brown goat cheese.

Italian Ricotta, much like cottage cheese, is used primarily for pastas and desserts.

No other cheese available in America is quite like Greek Feta, which is snow-white, salty, and crumbly but sliceable. Good with olives, Feta may be eaten with either fingers or forks, or used in cooked dishes.

Cold Salmon Buffet

FOR TWELVE PEOPLE

WHOLE SALMON WITH TARRAGON DRESSING

GREEN BEAN AND ONION SALAD

BREAD TRAY

MIXED SUMMER FRUITS

This cold buffet, featuring a whole salmon, is a do-ahead meal. The menu is appropriate for serving either indoors or outdoors, depending on the weather and your serving facilities. You will need to do most of your preparations a day ahead or early in the day you serve, as the fish and salad must chill.

WHOLE SALMON WITH TARRAGON DRESSING

A cold baked salmon with head and tail left on provides the attractive entrée for this buffet dinner. You can bake the fish as much as a day ahead and finish preparations several hours before serving.

A 6 to 8-pound piece of halibut or giant sea bass may be used instead of the salmon. A tapered piece from the tail end of the fish will look best when served, and will fit on the baking pan in one piece. If more than about 3½ inches thick, the piece may take 15 to 20 minutes longer to bake. Serve as directed for the salmon.

1	whole salmon, 6 to 8 pounds
1	teaspoon salt
	Dash pepper
3	tablespoons butter or margarine
½	small head lettuce
2	cups mayonnaise (or use half sour cream)
1	tablespoon crushed tarragon
2	tablespoons lemon juice
1	tablespoon minced onion
¾	teaspoon salt
¼	teaspoon pepper
	Lemon slices, cherry tomatoes, parsley for garnish

Have fish cleaned but don't remove head and tail. Sprinkle 1 teaspoon salt and dash pepper inside fish; dot with butter. Cut fish in half crosswise.

Cover an 11 by 15-inch shallow baking pan with lettuce leaves and place both halves of the fish on the lettuce. Bake uncovered in a 400° oven for 1 hour or until fish flakes easily. Cool, then chill several hours or overnight.

To make the mask, mix mayonnaise (or mayonnaise and sour cream), tarragon, lemon juice, onion, ¾ teaspoon salt, and ¼ teaspoon pepper; chill.

To serve the fish, put the two halves together again on a large serving platter. (You may need to cut a thin slice from each cut end to allow the two halves to fit together neatly.) Then spread half of the mayonnaise mixture over the surface of the fish, leaving the head and tail exposed. Spoon the remaining mayonnaise mixture into a bowl to serve with the fish.

For the first servings, cut down only to the backbone of the salmon; when the top half has been completely served, carefully remove the spine and adjoining bones. The bottom side of the fish is then ready for second servings with the extra dressing. Garnish the whole fish with lemon slices, cherry tomatoes, and parsley. Makes 12 servings.

GREEN BEANS AND ONION SALAD

4	packages (9 oz. each) frozen green beans
½	cup water
1	sweet onion
½	cup salad oil
½	teaspoon each salt and oregano
	Dash pepper
2	tablespoons each white wine vinegar and lemon juice

Cook beans in water until tender; drain. Thinly slice onion and add to beans. Combine salad oil, salt, oregano, and pepper; pour over beans and onions. Refrigerate the salad overnight or until well chilled. Just before serving, stir in vinegar and lemon juice. Mix thoroughly. Spoon into serving dish, draining off most of the marinade. Makes 12 servings.

French Peasant Aïoli

FRENCH PEASANT AÏOLI

AÏOLI SAUCE

HOT OR COLD SEAFOOD, VEGETABLES, EGGS

FRENCH BREAD

The people of Provence on the southeastern coastal area of France make a whole meal of crusty bread, seafood, vegetables, and a garlic mayonnaise sauce called Aïoli (pronounced "eye-o-lee"). This golden sauce reeks of garlic. But its flavor is an exciting experience once one gets past the aroma, and an enhancement to plain accompaniments.

Indications are that Aïoli Sauce came from the Greeks, who still have a similar garlic sauce by that name, thickened with bread crumbs, walnuts, or potatoes, rather than egg as the French version is. The transfer of name as well as flavor to France probably occurred in the dim past when Greek colonists populated the French southern coast. Or it may have happened when the Romans, who prized Greek cooking and its civilized refinements, moved in later.

Aïoli is the name of both the sauce and the meal made from dipping the seafood and vegetables in this sauce. Below are a number of suggested foods, but there is no reason why you can't simplify the dish for a light luncheon by serving just two or three foods—such as shrimp, whole artichokes, and hard-cooked eggs.

To prepare an Aïoli Meal. The array you present as Aïoli can be freely chosen from locally available fish, shellfish, and vegetables—but no meat.

Since the meal is typically peasant-style and help-yourself, you have great latitude in presenting the food. If you serve it from the center of a big roomy table, with knives and cutting boards handy to all, you can leave the foods whole and handsome, letting guests break or cut them up to eat. For buffet service, dishing up is simplified if the larger pieces of vegetables and fish are precut, then reassembled to preserve their appearance. For individual service, you can arrange an assortment of Aïoli ingredients like a still life picture, on a plate.

The cooked foods that Aïoli Sauce complements might include the following:

Hot boiled new potatoes
Hot or cold cooked green beans
 and artichokes
Cold cooked shrimp and lobster
 (remove lobster meat, cut, and
 return to shell)

Hot or cold poached halibut,
 lingcod, or other lean white
 fish (served whole if possible)
Hard cooked eggs

The following raw vegetables are suitable:

Fennel (also called sweet anise
 or finocchio)
Red or white cabbage (cut or to
 be cut in wedges)
Cherry tomatoes or regular
 tomatoes (to be cut in
 wedges)
Mushrooms
Turnips and zucchini (sliced
 partly through to snap apart)
Cauliflower
Green peppers (seeded if
 desired)
Belgian endive
Small inner romaine leaves

AÏOLI SAUCE

6	to 8 medium-sized or 4 large garlic cloves
1½	tablespoons lemon juice
½	teaspoon salt
3	egg yolks
½	cup salad oil
½	cup olive oil
1	to 2 tablespoons water

Force garlic through a garlic press and combine in a bowl with lemon juice, salt, and egg yolks. Beat with a rotary beater or wire whip until blended. Add oil a few drops at a time, beating rapidly and constantly. When sauce thickens, you can add more oil, but no faster than it can be easily mixed in. Thin with water if needed.

Chill sauce, covered, for at least several hours to mellow flavor. Makes 1¾ cups.

Shellfish on Ice

ASSORTED SHELLFISH ON ICE

VARIETY OF SEAFOOD SAUCES

ABALONE SEVICHE

CAESAR SALAD

ITALIAN BREAD STICKS AND SWEET BUTTER

HOT AND COLD BEVERAGES

Because you can buy the shellfish already cooked when necessary, this can be an almost effortless company dinner. Mix the sauces in advance, in a blender or by hand. The salad calls for quick last-minute showmanship.

This party menu is particularly adaptable to serving out of doors; choose a cool protected spot with a lush green background. A small rustic plank or glass-topped table holds the buffet supper. You might seat guests at a large patio table or supply trays for lap service.

Containers holding the iced shellfish should be deep enough to hold the water from the melting cracked or crushed ice. Wooden soy tubs are ideal for icing both the shellfish and the wine or other chilled beverages; colorful metal serving dishes or trays with raised edges could also be used.

Selecting and Preparing the Shellfish. For the entrees, choose the shellfish you think your guests would like best. For example, to serve eight persons, you might purchase the following: 4 Alaskan king crab legs (approximately 2 pounds); 2 or 3 Dungeness crabs, cooked and cracked; 1 or 2 spiny lobsters, cooked and split in half; 1½ to 2 dozen Eastern blue point oysters, rock cockle or cherrystone clams, raw on the half shell; 3 pounds prawns, counting 8 to 10 to the pound, or the small local ocean shrimp, cooked; and 1 pound thinly sliced raw abalone for the Abalone Seviche.

The shellfish do not require any special preparations, but be sure to scrub them thoroughly while they are still encased in the shell. Break the king crab legs at the joints into serving-size pieces; with kitchen scissors, cut off half of the shell along the sides to reveal the crab meat, then serve the meat in the remaining half shell. Remove the lobster meat from the half shells and cut into inch-wide pieces; return to the shell. The oysters or clams on the half shell, the large whole prawns, and the cracked Dungeness crabs are ready for serving as is.

Embed the shells of crab, lobster, oysters, and clams in the ice. Small shrimp and the Abalone Seviche may be in bowls or shells embedded to the rim.

SEAFOOD SAUCES

Here are four smoothly seasoned sauces to accompany seafood, served either in the shell or as traditional seafood cocktails. Lemon Butter Mayonnaise is excellent with lobster, prawns, Dungeness crab, and Alaskan king crab meat. Spicy Cocktail Sauce goes with oysters, clams, and prawns. Green Mayonnaise suits lobster and crab. Remoulade Sauce complements all but oysters and clams.

LEMON BUTTER MAYONNAISE. In the container of your blender combine 3 egg yolks, 1 teaspoon grated lemon peel, 2 tablespoons lemon juice, 1 tablespoon white wine vinegar, ¾ teaspoon sugar, 2 teaspoons Dijon-style mustard, and ½ teaspoon salt; whirl at high speed for 30 seconds. With motor turned on at high speed, add in a slow steady stream ½ cup *each* salad oil and melted butter (cooled to lukewarm). As mixture thickens, turn blender off frequently and blend oil in with a rubber spatula. Serve at room temperature.

To make the mayonnaise with a mixer, combine all ingredients but oil and butter; beat at high speed for 30 seconds. While beating at high speed, add oil and butter in a slow steady stream. This mayonnaise is thinner than that made in a blender, but you can chill it to thicken. Makes about 1¾ cups.

SPICY COCKTAIL SAUCE. Mix together just until blended 1 cup chile sauce, ½ teaspoon Worcestershire, 4 drops liquid hot-pepper seasoning, and ⅓ cup lemon juice. Cover and chill. Makes 1⅓ cups sauce.

GREEN MAYONNAISE. Mix together ¼ cup mayonnaise, ½ cup sour cream, 2 teaspoons lemon juice, ⅛ teaspoon crumbled dried tarragon, ¼ teaspoon salt, and 1 clove garlic, mashed. Mix in ¼ cup *each* finely chopped watercress, spinach, and parsley. Cover and chill. Makes about 1½ cups sauce.

REMOULADE SAUCE. Mix together 2 tablespoons *each* finely chopped chives, capers, dill pickle, and parsley into 1 cup mayonnaise. Makes about 1½ cups.

ABALONE SEVICHE

This abalone marinated in lime juice "cooks" without benefit of heat.

    1   pound thinly sliced raw abalone
    6   tablespoons lime juice
    2   tablespoons salad oil
    ½   cup canned green chile salsa
    ¼   teaspoon each salt, pepper, and garlic salt
    ½   teaspoon sugar
    3   drops liquid hot-pepper seasoning
        Thinly sliced lime

Cut abalone into strips about 1 inch wide and 1½ inches long, and place in a small bowl. Mix together the lime juice, salad oil, chile salsa, salt, pepper, garlic salt, sugar, and hot-pepper seasoning. Pour sauce over the abalone and mix well; then cover and refrigerate for about 4 hours or overnight. At serving time, spoon into an abalone shell or other serving container, and garnish with lime, thinly sliced. Furnish toothpicks for serving. Makes 8 servings.

CAESAR SALAD

This classic dinner salad can also become a hot weather entrée if you enrich it with meat, seafood, or poultry. For a main-dish salad or 4 to 6 servings, increase the total quantity of cheese to ⅔ cup, and use a total of 2 cups croutons.

You can add any *one* of the following meats and seafood: ⅔ pound cooked meat, thinly sliced and cut in ½-inch strips (salami, corned beef, boiled ham, roast beef); 2 cans (5 or 6 oz *each*) shrimp or lobster, rinsed and drained. Add meat or seafood when you toss in the croutons.

    1   clove garlic
    2   large heads romaine lettuce
    ½   cup olive oil
    2   eggs, simmered 1 minute
        Juice of 1 lemon (3 tablespoons juice)
    8   anchovy fillets, chopped
    ⅓   cup grated Parmesan cheese
    1   cup toasted garlic croutons
        Salt and pepper to taste

Rub salad bowl with a crushed clove of garlic. Break romaine into bite-sized pieces and turn into the bowl. Pour over oil, and mix greens until well coated. Break the eggs into the salad and mix. Sprinkle with lemon juice and mix thoroughly. Add anchovies and cheese and mix again. Add the croutons and mix well. Taste; season with salt and pepper to taste. Serve at once. Makes 8 servings.

Fruit and Cheese Snack Tray

FRUIT AND CHEESE SNACK TRAY

POMEGRANATE CHEESE LOAF

MELBA TOAST OR CRISP CRACKERS

CRÈME DE MENTHE GRAPES

PISTACHIO PINEAPPLE FINGERS

HONEYED FIGS

This fruit and cheese tray can serve as a snack for informal get-togethers when guests drop over for an hour or two in late afternoon or after dinner.

Everything can be served on one large tray, and everything is a finger food—but be sure to have plenty of small paper napkins handy for eating the juicy figs. Many kinds of bever-

ages can be served with this snack, including a special coffee (see page 62), spiced tea, fruit juice, punch, carbonated beverages, Sherry, Port, or Vermouth.

POMEGRANATE CHEESE LOAF

You can make the cheese mixture several days before shaping and serving.

1	*package (8 oz.) cream cheese (at room temperature)*
⅛	*pound Roquefort cheese*
½	*pound Cheddar cheese spread or Cheddar, shredded*
	Pomegranate seeds (optional)

Blend cheeses together until smooth. Chill thoroughly, then shape into a loaf or ball. Dot surface with pomegranate seeds and chill until ready to serve.

CRÈME DE MENTHE GRAPES

Divide a medium-sized bunch of seedless grapes into small clusters; wash and drain thoroughly. Dip each cluster into a small amount of crème de menthe. Dust grapes generously with powdered sugar, place on a baking sheet, and set in the freezer or freezing compartment of your refrigerator for 25 to 30 minutes. Then refrigerate until ready to serve. Arrange grapes on tray and sprinkle lightly with powdered sugar, if desired. Instead of crème de menthe, you can dip the grapes in egg white, slightly beaten, then sprinkle with powdered sugar.

PISTACHIO PINEAPPLE FINGERS

Cut fresh pineapple into small fingers, or use canned spears. Dip one end of each piece in finely chopped pistachios. Arrange on tray; chill until ready to use.

HONEYED FIGS

Choose well-shaped, dried light (Calimyrna) figs, and chill for 2 or 3 hours in a mixture of half honey, half Port. Serve figs in a small dish of the honey and Port on the cheese tray.

GOOD MORNING BREAKFASTS FOR GUESTS

Usually you have time to plan ahead for breakfast guests, but not always. Sometimes they are people you invite to stay overnight after a late party, out-of-town visitors who breeze in unannounced, or good friends you suddenly decide to join for a fishing or ski trip.

Breakfast menus are fairly standard—usually fruit or juice, eggs, breakfast meats, and bread or pastry, often with some sweetness. When you can plan in advance for a special breakfast, it is possible to bake sweet breads or do something a little different with meat. However, for impromptu occasions your best bet is to dress up the eggs in some fashion and make a favorite kind of pancake.

Following are easy ways to make eggs with a company touch (some even include the breakfast meat).

Baked Eggs in Tomato Shells. Scoop out the pulp and drain 4 medium-sized tomatoes (save the pulp and juice for use later in a sauce). Sprinkle the inside of each tomato shell with a dash of salt, pepper, and basil. Break 4 eggs, one at a time, into a small dish and gently slip one into each tomato. Bake in a 350° oven for about 20 minutes, or until eggs are almost set to the degree of doneness you prefer. Sprinkle each with 1 teaspoon grated Parmesan cheese and place under the broiler until cheese is just bubbly. Garnish with a sprig of parsley.

Scotch Eggs. Hard-cook 8 small or medium eggs and remove shells. With your hands, flatten 1¼ pounds pork sausage meat on a floured board, and cut into eight pieces. Mold meat around each egg, rolling it around with your hands until the egg is completely covered. Dip sausage-covered eggs in 1 egg, slightly beaten, then in fine dry bread crumbs (about ¾ cup), and deep fry in moderately hot fat (about 370°) for 4 to 5 minutes, or until sausage is deep brown.

Corned Beef Hash and Egg Cups. Spoon canned corned beef hash into buttered custard cups, or cups shaped from heavy foil. Make a hollow in the center; drop in an egg, dot with butter, sprinkle with salt and pepper, and add 1 teaspoon whipping cream. Bake in a 375° oven for 15 to 20 minutes, or until whites are just firm. A 1-pound can of corned beef hash will make about 6 servings.

Baked Eggs and Sausages. For each serving, butter 1 custard cup and add a sprinkle of chervil or summer savory to each. Carefully crack 1 egg into each cup and top with 1 teaspoon light cream. Sprinkle with salt and paprika. Arrange 2 precooked tiny link sausages in each cup. Bake in a 350° oven for 12 to 15 minutes, or until whites are just firm.

Portuguese Country Dinner

FOR FOUR PEOPLE (RECIPES EASILY DOUBLED OR TREBLED)

CARNE DE PORCO CON VINHA D'ALHOS

Country-style spareribs in garlic wine

PURÊ DE BATATAS

Mashed potatoes (use your favorite method)

COUVE CON CEBOLAS

Swiss chard, mustard, or kale with onions

COMPOTA DE MAÇÃ

Applesauce (canned or freshly made)

SALADA

Crisp lettuce with sweetened vinegar dressing

SUSPIROS

Traditional meringue cooky dessert

This Portuguese dinner is simple and wholesome, and the foods are inexpensive; only the seasonings will strike you as being a little unusual. Since the complete meal can be on the table at one time, serving is simple.

Pork is the main dish in this meal based on authentic Portuguese recipes. Meaty country-style spareribs marinate for several days in a particularly mild and aromatic version of vinha d'alhos, freely translated "garlic wine." Then the ribs are roasted and the good brown drippings are ladled on mashed potatoes. Plain, unspiced applesauce offsets the richness of the pork.

PORTUGUESE SPARERIBS IN GARLIC WINE

These ribs marinate four days in vinegar and spices and, when baked, have a hearty, nose-tickling aroma.

4	pounds country-style spareribs
1	cup cider vinegar
3	cups water
½	cup dry white wine
2	teaspoons each crushed whole coriander and crushed whole cumin
5	to 6 cloves garlic
¼	teaspoon cayenne
2	teaspoons salt
½	cup water
4	to 6 tablespoons water

Put spareribs in a deep glass or ceramic bowl. Blend together vinegar, 3 cups water, wine, coriander, cumin, garlic cloves (slightly broken), cayenne, and salt. Pour liquid over pork. Cover and refrigerate for 4 days; turn meat in marinade several times.

On the fourth day, remove meat from marinade and let drain for about 30 minutes. Discard all liquid. Arrange meat in a single layer in a roasting pan and add ½ cup water. Bake uncovered in a 350° oven for 2 hours. Remove to a serving platter. Skim as much fat as possible from drippings, then add 4 to 6 tablespoons water to pan and bring to a boil, scraping free all the browned particles. Serve separately in a sauce dish. Cut between ribs to serve meat; it may require additional salt to taste. Makes 4 servings.

GREENS WITH ONIONS

Wash and coarsely chop enough Swiss chard, kale, or mustard greens (including stems if you use Swiss chard) to make 10 cups, lightly packed. Thinly slice 2 medium-sized onions and cook in a wide pan over moderate heat in 2 tablespoons salad oil or melted butter, stirring occasionally, until browned. Add the greens and ½ cup water. Cover and cook for about 10 minutes, stirring occasionally; or cook until greens are tender. Season with salt.

SALAD WITH VINEGAR DRESSING

Mix 2 tablespoons vinegar with 2 teaspoons sugar. Sprinkle this over about 4 cups broken iceberg lettuce, then toss. If you like, add sliced tomatoes or green pepper rings for a little extra color and fresh flavor, plus salt and pepper to taste.

SUSPIROS

The name of these Portuguese meringue cookies means "sighs." They are soft as a sigh and very sigh-inspiring. They may be made several days ahead, but they must be kept in an airtight container until serving time.

    3   egg whites
    ⅛   teaspoon cream of tartar
    ½   cup sugar

Beat egg whites with cream of tartar until whites are thick and foamy. Gradually add sugar, beating constantly. Continue whipping until whites are stiff enough to hold high peaks that curl downward.

Force meringue through a pastry bag fitted with a fancy tip (or drop by generous teaspoonfuls) onto baking sheets lined with brown paper or other special baking-pan lining paper. Leave about an inch between each cooky. Bake in a 325° oven for 30 minutes or until an even gold in color. Carefully remove cookies from paper immediately, using a spatula, and cool on wire racks. Cookies must be sealed airtight (such as in a heavy plastic bag) until serving time if prepared ahead. Makes 1½ to 2 dozen cookies.

Supper Beside the Fire

FOR FOUR PEOPLE

BARBECUED SIRLOIN WITH PARSLEY HERB BUTTER

GRILLED FRENCH FRIES

BUTTER LETTUCE SALAD

FRENCH ROLLS

ALTERNATE 1: FLAMING RUM BABAS

ALTERNATE 2: COFFEE MOLD WITH FLAMING NUT SAUCE

When you gather a few friends around the fireplace at home to cook your supper and eat there, a successful evening with stimulating or merry conversation is almost guaranteed. The setting provides two elements seldom combined—glamor and informality. To further the warm glow if the weather is wet or icy, you can serve hot drinks or punch. The flaming dessert also contributes to the cozy yet elegant mood.

Prepare for the fire and cooking equipment ahead. For flamefree cooking that is easy to control, use charcoal briquets instead of wood. If your grate has an open shape that will not hold charcoal, you can make an impromptu grate with a piece of fine-mesh hardware cloth. Cut the piece about 16 by 24 inches in size and bend up each side about 1½ inches; place on top of grate or andirons.

An inexpensive, collapsible camp grill, available in hardware stores, makes a fine cooking surface for barbecuing steak and supporting other foods while cooking or heating.

Cook the steak and French fries simultaneously over the coals. To make potatoes for four people, place 2 packages (8 oz. each) frozen French-fried potatoes in a popcorn popper or other wire basket; place on grill over coals, shaking occasionally, for 10 to 15 minutes, or until browned and cooked.

Heat the rolls in a heavy foil pan, if you like. Serve 1 can (12 oz.) rum babas, heated in their own syrup in a foil pan on the grill; if you wish, flame them with 2 tablespoons rum. If you choose the molded coffee ice cream, make the sauce and prepare the mold ahead using ready-made ice cream. At serving time, all you do is unmold it onto a chilled plate and top with flaming sauce.

BARBECUED SIRLOIN WITH HERB BUTTER

    One-inch-thick top sirloin steak (about 2 lbs.)
½   *cup chopped parsley*
2   *cloves garlic*
3   *green onions, white part only*
½   *cup butter*
2   *teaspoons lemon juice*
1   *teaspoon each anchovy paste and Dijon-style mustard*

Place steak over coals on a grill and barbecue on both sides, allowing about 4 to 5 minutes on a side for rare meat. Cut in 4 servings and serve with this parsley herb butter:

Finely chop together parsley, garlic, and the white part of the green onions. Heat butter and stir in lemon juice, anchovy paste, and Dijon-style mustard. Remove the herb butter from the heat and stir in the minced greens. Makes 1 cup sauce. The steak will serve 4 people.

COFFEE MOLD WITH FLAMING NUT SAUCE

Let ½ gallon coffee ice cream soften slightly; then pack into a fancy 2-quart metal mold, cover with foil, and return to the freezer for at least 2 hours, or until solidly frozen. When ready to serve, dip mold in hottest tap water for about 10 seconds, then turn upside down on a large chilled plate. Return to the freezer while preparing sauce.

Coarsely chop ¾ cup Brazil nuts. Melt 2 tablespoons butter in a small serving pan, add nut meats, and brown them lightly. Warm ¼ cup brandy slightly.

Assemble the dessert at the table before guests. First spoon out a tablespoon of the warmed brandy, ignite, and pour it over the nut meats in the pan. Then pour the remaining brandy over the nuts and spoon the flaming sauce over the ice cream. Makes 10 servings.

A Patio Buffet

FOR EIGHT PEOPLE

HERBED LEG OF LAMB WITH ROASTED POTATOES

COLD BROCCOLI WITH CASHEWS

FRESH CUCUMBER MOLD

CROISSANTS

ORANGE CHEDDAR CHEESECAKE

Except for the roasting of the leg of lamb and potatoes together in the oven, last-minute preparation for this dinner is almost eliminated.

Everything is served cold except the entrée. You can prepare the cucumber mold and the cheesecake the day before the party, and the broccoli up to 8 hours before serving time.

HERBED LEG OF LAMB

You might try lamb cooked the classic French way—medium rare or medium well done instead of well done. Bring the leg of lamb to the table on a carving board, garnished attractively.

5½	to 6-pound leg of lamb
2	cloves garlic
1	tablespoon dry mustard
2	teaspoons salt
⅛	teaspoon pepper
½	teaspoon whole thyme
¼	teaspoon crushed rosemary
1	tablespoon lemon juice
10	to 12 medium-sized potatoes, peeled
	Butter
2	tablespoons flour
	Water

Rub all surfaces of lamb with 1 clove garlic, peeled and halved. Cut this clove and 1 more into slivers. Slit skin of lamb at intervals over the top surface; insert slivered garlic into slits. Blend dry mustard, salt, pepper, thyme, rosemary, and lemon juice. Spread over surface of the roast. Coat potatoes well with butter; place in pan with roast.

Place lamb on rack in an uncovered roasting pan in a 325° oven and roast for 2 to 2½ hours or longer, until thermometer in thickest part registers 150° (for medium rare); 160° (medium well done); or 175° (well done). Baste occasionally with pan drippings.

Remove meat and potatoes to platter; keep warm. For sauce, skim fat from pan drippings; reserve 1 tablespoon. Stir flour into fat in pan; heat until bubbly. Add water to skimmed drippings to make 1½ cups; blend into flour mixture, stirring constantly until thickened. Simmer for 3 to 5 minutes; strain to remove crusty particles. Makes 6 to 8 servings.

COLD BROCCOLI WITH CASHEWS

Cold vegetables are always good on a summer menu, as they can serve as both salad and vegetable. The broccoli can be prepared up to 8 hours ahead and chilled until serving time.

3	pounds broccoli
½	cup olive oil
¼	cup lemon juice
½	teaspoon salt
	Dash pepper
2	teaspoons chervil
½	cup salted cashews, coarsely broken

Cook the broccoli until it is just tender; place in a serving dish. Combine the olive oil, lemon juice, salt, pepper, and chervil. Pour over the broccoli; chill. Just before serving, sprinkle with cashews. Makes 8 servings.

FRESH CUCUMBER MOLD

Puréed cucumbers are the base of this rich and delicate mold. You can prepare it a day in advance.

2	envelopes unflavored gelatin
½	cup water
4	medium-sized cucumbers
¾	cup each sour cream and mayonnaise
2½	tablespoons prepared horseradish
2	tablespoons grated onion
1	teaspoon salt
¼	teaspoon white pepper
1	cup heavy cream, whipped
	Oil
	Thinly sliced cucumbers
	Watercress

Soften gelatin in ½ cup water, and place over hot water to dissolve. Pare cucumbers, cut in half lengthwise, and remove seeds. Chop cucumbers and whirl in blender to make a smooth purée. Measure 3 cups purée and combine with sour cream, mayonnaise, horseradish, onion, salt, and white pepper. Stir in the dissolved gelatin. Chill until thickened (about 45 minutes). Fold in whipped cream. Turn into a lightly oiled 1½-quart salad mold. Chill at least 4 hours or until set. Unmold and garnish with thinly sliced cucumbers and watercress. Makes 8 servings.

ORANGE CHEDDAR CHEESECAKE

Grated citrus peels add zest to the unusual blend of Cheddar cheese and beer in this variation on traditional cheesecake.

1	cup crushed orange-flavored cooky wafers
2	tablespoons melted butter
2	large packages (8 oz. each) cream cheese, softened
½	cup finely shredded Cheddar cheese
¾	cup sugar
2	tablespoons flour
3	eggs
¼	cup beer
¼	cup whipping cream
¼	teaspoon each grated orange peel and grated lemon peel
½	teaspoon vanilla

Mix the cooky crumbs with the melted butter and pat into the bottom of a buttered 9-inch cheesecake pan (one with removable bottom or spring-release sides). Bake in a 350° oven for 8 minutes. Whip the cream cheese until light and fluffy and blend in the Cheddar cheese. Gradually beat in the ¾ cup sugar mixed with the flour. Add eggs, one at a time, beating until smooth. Mix in the beer and cream. Add the grated orange and lemon peels and vanilla, mixing well. Turn into crumb-lined pan; bake in a 350° oven for 30 minutes. Cool, then chill. Makes 10 servings.

A Wine-Tasting

MELON OR PAPAYA WITH PROSCIUTTO OR HAM

APPETIZER WINE

ICED SHRIMP IN DILL MARINADE

RYE WAFER BREAD

WHITE WINE

SLICED TOMATOES WITH CAPERS

ROSÉ WINE

PASTA A PESTO

COLD ROAST BEEF

RED WINE

BEL PAESE CHEESE, CRUSTY BREAD, FRUIT

DESSERT WINE

Have all the food ready before guests are due, and the wines at the prescribed temperature. The dessert course of cheese, bread, and fruit can be in place on the buffet as decoration through the meal.

Bring on the other foods, wines, and glasses (chilled if to be served with chilled wine) in order of eating. Have the table or tables set with individual places.

Selecting the Wines. For the appetizer wine, serve either sweet or dry Vermouth (a blended wine flavored with herbs) over ice cubes.

For the white wine to accompany the iced shrimp, select dry, tart Rhine wine; serve well chilled. Among Rhine types are Johannisberg and White Riesling.

The light pink rosé, with fruity flavor, should be served chilled. If made from the Grenache grape, this wine will be labeled Grenache Rosé.

The red dinner wine to accompany the pasta should be a ruby-colored Claret served at cool room temperature or very lightly chilled. Good wines in the Claret category may be labeled Zinfandel or Cabernet Sauvignon.

The dessert wine may be one of the sweet wines made from muscat grapes, such as Muscat de Frontignan, Light

Sweet Muscat, or Black Muscat. All these retain some of the flavor of the grape; they may be served chilled or at room temperature. If muscat wines are not available, you may substitute Port.

One bottle of each kind of wine is sufficient per 6 to 8 people.

Preparing the Foods. For the appetizer, top slender wedges of chilled Crenshaw melon or papaya with paper-thin slices of prosciutto (cured ham available in Italian delicatessens). If the prosciutto is not readily available, you can substitute very thinly sliced pastrami, plain baked ham, or Westphalian ham.

To prepare tomatoes for 8 people, select about 4 large tomatoes and peel if desired. Cut in thick slices and arrange on a tray with 3 or 4 hard-cooked eggs, cut in wedges. Garnish with tender lettuce leaves. Sprinkle liberally with coarsely chopped capers (about 1½ tablespoons) and drizzle with olive oil (about 2 tablespoons). Sprinkle the tomatoes very lightly with salt, and grind black pepper over the vegetables.

You may roast your own beef or buy slices from a delicatessen.

ICED SHRIMP IN DILL MARINADE

A marinade seasoned with lemon juice, dill weed, minced onion, and allspice flavors the shrimp, which can be prepared well in advance.

2	pounds large shrimp or prawns (about 40 to the pound)
	Boiling salted water
¾	cup stock from boiled shrimp
½	cup lemon juice
1	teaspoon dill weed
3	tablespoons minced onion
2	teaspoons sugar
1	teaspoon salt
¼	teaspoon ground allspice
	Fresh dill or parsley sprigs (optional)
	Lemon wedges
	Rye wafer bread

Devein shrimp (see note below); drop in boiling salted water. Cook until shrimp turn bright pink. Drain; reserve ¾ cup of the stock. Shell shrimp and pour marinade over them. To make marinade, mix ¾ cup stock with lemon juice, dill weed, onion, sugar, 1 teaspoon salt, and allspice. Cover and chill for at least 4 hours (or overnight). Serve shrimp from a well-chilled iced container. Garnish, if you like, with fresh dill or parsley sprigs. Serve with lemon wedges and rye wafer bread. Makes 6 servings.

Note: To devein shrimp without shelling, insert a slender wooden or metal skewer into the back of each shrimp just below the vein and gently pull to surface; repeat several times as required for each shrimp.

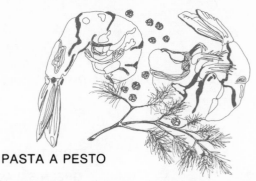

PASTA A PESTO

This sauce for the pasta can be made several weeks ahead. To serve, you may wish to toss noodles with sauce in a chafing dish.

¼	cup dried basil (or 1 cup of fresh leaves)
¼	cup chopped fresh parsley
1	or 2 small cloves garlic
⅔	cup olive oil
¼	teaspoon nutmeg
1	cup lightly packed, freshly grated Parmesan or Romano cheese
1	teaspoon salt
1	pound tagliarini (or other flat ribbon noodle)

With a blender, or a mortar and pestle, reduce the basil, parsley, and garlic to a pulp, slowly adding olive oil to make a smooth paste. Add nutmeg, cheese, and 1 teaspoon salt. Cook noodles in a large amount of boiling salted water until tender. Drain, add basil sauce, and toss until well coated.

If you want to use a chafing dish, toss noodles with sauce in the dish over direct flame. Serve immediately, or cover and keep in the hot water bath of the chafing dish. Makes 6 to 8 servings.

HOW TO HAVE A WINE-TASTING

At a wine-tasting party, the wine not only is the beverage but the entertainment as well. Nearly everyone is curious about wines and delighted to have a chance to try new kinds. A tasting provides a good setting for mixing people who do not know each other. The wines give reason for striking up a conversation, and people must mill about if the bottles are set up on different tables.

The most simple tasting, with four to six kinds of wine to try, may be accompanied by an assortment of cheeses and crackers or good bread. You may want to combine a cheese-tasting with the wine-tasting. Allow a minimum of a half bottle of wine *total* per guest.

A more sophisticated tasting may offer an array of appetizers designed to complement the wines offered. Seafood and vegetable appetizers may be served with white wines; pâtés, meats, and stronger cheeses with the reds. Although being too much of a purist about foods served with wine at most meals is not advisable, you should choose those

for a tasting which let the wines shine. Vinegar, heavy spice, asparagus, citrus fruits, strong or salty dips, and strong fish are best avoided.

Obviously a wine-tasting may be a complete meal—at the table or buffet-style. For a buffet tasting, arrange wines and accompanying foods in order on a long table, or set up each course on a separate table.

The choice of wines for comparison at tastings may be made several ways. You might choose to have two appetizer wines, two whites, two reds, and two dessert wines so that comparison can be made at each stage. Or the tasting can be devoted solely to whites, reds, or Sherry if you would like to get to know one type in depth. You could make your tasting even more narrow, sampling various brands of California Burgundies made from just the Pinot Noir grape. Or you can make comparisons between several California and European wines of the same type.

The Fondue Party

RECIPES MAKE FOUR MAIN-DISH SERVINGS, OR TWELVE TO SIXTEEN APPETIZER SERVINGS

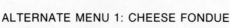

ALTERNATE MENU 1: CHEESE FONDUE

GREEN SALAD OR FRUIT SALAD

ALTERNATE MENU 2: BEEF FONDUE

SAUCES AND SEASONED BUTTERS

BAKED POTATOES AND FRENCH BREAD

GREEN SALAD

ALTERNATE MENU 3: SEAFOOD FONDUE

AVOCADO SAUCE, CHUTNEY SAUCE

BAKED OR PARSLEY BUTTERED POTATOES

COLE SLAW OR CAESAR SALAD

Caesar Salad recipe on page 84

Guests enjoy the do-it-yourself aspect of preparing and eating fondue. Special fondue pots, each with its own stand and heating unit, are available in a variety of styles. You can use an electric frying pan for the meat or seafood types.

The Cheese Fondue Party. Once you've mastered making Cheese Fondue, you can serve this dish for many informal occasions, either as an appetizer or main course.

Each guest spears a piece of bread with a fork. He dips it in the pot, gives it a good stir (fondue needs to be stirred continuously), then twirls bread and cheese in the air until it stops dripping and cools.

By setting up several small tables, each with its own pot of fondue, you can provide for larger groups. The number of guests is limited only by the tables, fondue pots, and heating units you can collect, and by the pre-party helpers you can recruit. Making each pot of fondue requires the full attention of one cook for about 30 minutes while the cheese is gradually stirred into the hot wine. You can have the cheese shredded, wine measured into the pots, and everything ready for your helpers to stir the ingredients together.

To encourage guests to mingle and change tables, mark each person's fondue fork and glass or cup with his initial so he can move about, carrying those utensils with him. Have a small plate at each place for keeping bread cubes ready to dip. Dry white wine (usually the same wine used in the fondue) or hot tea is the only accompaniment needed.

Halfway through this feast, it is traditional to offer small

glasses of kirsch (cherry brandy), which is said to promote digestion and stimulate the appetite.

As the quantity of fondue diminishes toward the end of the meal, the cheese tends to stick a little and form a crust on the bottom. In Switzerland, where this dish originated, the crust is considered a special delicacy.

After the fondue, you could serve either a green salad with oil and vinegar dressing or light fruit salad—or just fruit for dessert.

The Beef or Seafood Fondue Party. Beef or seafood fondue differs from cheese fondue in that the pot contains bubbling butter and oil into which you dip cubes of steak, fish, or whole shrimp to cook them. After the cooking, which takes just a minute or two, you then swirl the chunks in little bowls of spicy sauce or flavored butter.

Like cheese fondue, the meat or seafood version may be used either for an entrée or an appetizer, and it can be adapted to serve either small or large groups. Beef or seafood fondue is quick and simple to prepare.

You will need a cooking utensil which can be regulated to keep heat of the butter and oil at about 425°. If you use the traditional fondue pot with alcohol burner, check the temperature with deep-fat thermometer or practice regulating the heat ahead of time. An electric sauce or frying pan can also be used. Be sure the cooking utensil is on a sturdy table, well centered, with the handle, if any, placed where it is not likely to be jarred.

CHEESE FONDUE

The recipe for Cheese Fondue is simple, but there are a few requirements. You must use the right cheese. Only *imported* Swiss and Gruyère reliably melt into the wine to make a smooth sauce.

Next in importance is the correct heat for melting the cheese—hot enough to keep it bubbling slowly, but not so hot that the cheese separates. You can melt the cheese in a heatproof earthenware dish directly over a denatured alcohol or canned heat flame. If you use a metal pan, place it over simmering water. Use a heating unit designed so you can regulate the heat.

Use a light, dry white wine of good quality for the fondue.

    1   clove garlic, cut in half
    2   cups light dry white wine (such as Riesling,
            Chablis, or Traminer)
    ½   pound imported Swiss cheese (Emmental),
            shredded
    ½   pound Swiss or Danish Gruyère (Samsoe),
            shredded
    1   tablespoon cornstarch
    1   teaspoon dry mustard (optional)
    3   tablespoons kirsch (optional)
        Freshly ground nutmeg and pepper, to taste
    1   small loaf French bread, cut in 1-inch cubes
            with some crust on each

Rub the fondue pot with the cut garlic. Add wine, and heat slowly until bubbles form and slowly rise to the surface. Combine the two cheeses, cornstarch, and mustard (if used). Add cheese mixture, a spoonful at a time; stir slowly and continuously until all the cheese is blended into a smooth sauce.

Stir in kirsch (if used) a tablespoon at a time, and again bring to a slow boil. (If the heat gets too high at any time, the fondue may separate.) Sprinkle with nutmeg and pepper. Take to table with bread cubes, and adjust heat so fondue keeps bubbling slowly.

If fondue gets too thick, thin with heated wine.

BEEF FONDUE

    2   to 2½ pounds boneless beef sirloin or
            tenderloin
        Melted butter and salad oil
        Dipping sauce and butters (recipes follow)

Cut the meat into bite-sized cubes and refrigerate until about 15 to 20 minutes before serving time.

Pour the melted butter and salad oil (equal amounts of each) into a Fondue Bourguignonne pot or an electric frying pan to a depth of 1½ to 2 inches. Heat just below the smoking point (about 425° in electric frying pan). When guests are seated and the butter-oil mixture reaches the correct temperature, start cooking. Each guest spears a cube of beef with a fork and holds it in the hot butter-oil until cooked,

about 1 to 2 minutes. (Caution guests not to taste meat while on the hot cooking forks.)

Dip beef in one of the following sauces:

TERIYAKI SAUCE. Blend together ⅓ cup *each* canned consommé and Sherry; ¼ cup chopped green onions; 3 tablespoons *each* soy sauce, lime juice, and honey; 1 clove garlic, mashed; and 2 teaspoons freshly grated ginger. Heat to boiling; serve hot or cold.

TOASTED ONION BUTTER. Combine 1 teaspoon toasted dried onions, ¼ teaspoon *each* salt and Worcestershire, and ½ cup softened butter. Let stand several hours to blend flavors.

BLUE CHEESE BUTTER. Mix 1 package (4 oz.) blue cheese with ½ cup softened butter. Let stand several hours to blend.

MUSTARD BUTTER. Mix ¼ cup prepared mustard and ½ cup softened butter. Let stand to blend flavors.

SEAFOOD FONDUE

    ½   pound each salmon steaks and swordfish
            steaks
    ¾   pound raw medium-sized shrimp
    ½   pound scallops
        Dipping sauces (recipes follow)
    3   lemons
    2   bananas
    ¾   cup butter
    1½ cups salad oil

Cut salmon and swordfish into ¾-inch squares, discarding skin and bones. Peel and devein shrimp. Arrange fish and shellfish on a tray in separate sections, cover with plastic film, and chill until cooking time. Spoon the avocado and chutney dipping sauces into small bowls and chill. Cut lemons into wedges, place in a bowl, and chill. Just before cooking, peel bananas and slice in 1-inch rounds. Sprinkle with lemon juice.

To cook, heat butter and oil in a fondue pot placed over an alcohol burner until it starts to bubble. Arrange tray of fish and condiment sauces alongside. Let each person spear a piece of fish, shellfish, or banana with a fondue fork or a skewer and dip into the bubbling fat to cook. When fish takes on a tinge of brown on its edges, it is usually done.

Dip morsels in one of the following sauces:

AVOCADO SAUCE. Mix 1 thawed can (8 oz.) frozen avocado dip (or 1 small avocado, peeled and puréed) with 4 drops liquid hot-pepper seasoning and 1 tablespoon lemon juice. Chill.

CHUTNEY SAUCE. Mix together ¾ cup sour cream; 1 teaspoon curry powder; and ¼ cup chutney, chopped or puréed in a blender. Chill.

Index